AFTER PROPHECY

SPRING JOURNAL BOOKS
STUDIES IN ARCHETYPAL PSYCHOLOGY SERIES

Series Editor
GREG MOGENSON

OTHER TITLES IN THE SERIES

THE COLLECTED ENGLISH PAPERS OF WOLFGANG GIEGERICH
VOL. 1: THE NEUROSIS OF PSYCHOLOGY: PRIMARY PAPERS TOWARDS
A CRITICAL PSYCHOLOGY
VOL. 2: TECHNOLOGY AND THE SOUL: FROM THE NUCLEAR BOMB
TO THE WORLD WIDE WEB
Wolfgang Giegerich

DIALECTICS & ANALYTICAL PSYCHOLOGY:
THE EL CAPITAN CANYON SEMINAR
Wolfgang Giegerich, David L. Miller, Greg Mogenson

RAIDS ON THE UNTHINKABLE:
FREUDIAN *AND* JUNGIAN PSYCHOANALYSES
Paul Kugler

NORTHERN GNOSIS: THOR, BALDR, AND THE VOLSUNGS IN THE
THOUGHT OF FREUD AND JUNG
Greg Mogenson

THE ESSENTIALS OF STYLE: A HANDBOOK FOR SEEING AND BEING SEEN
Benjamin Sells

THE WOUNDED RESEARCHER: A DEPTH PSYCHOLOGICAL
APPROACH TO RESEARCH
Robert Romanyshyn

THE SUNKEN QUEST, THE WASTED FISHER, THE PREGNANT FISH:
POSTMODERN REFLECTIONS ON DEPTH PSYCHOLOGY
Ronald Schenk

FIRE IN THE STONE: THE ALCHEMY OF DESIRE
Stanton Marlan, ed.

AFTER PROPHECY

Imagination, Incarnation, and the Unity of the Prophetic Tradition

Lectures for the Temenos Academy

Tom Cheetham

Spring Journal Books
New Orleans, Louisiana

Published by
Spring Journal, Inc.;
627 Ursulines Street #7
New Orleans, Louisiana 70116
Tel.: (504) 810-2945
Website: www.springjournalandbooks.com

Cover design by
Michael Mendis
24 Blackfriars Street
London, Ont. N6H 1K6
Canada

Cover photograph:
Abbey Church of San Galgano, Tuscany (c. 1224-28)
Courtesy of Jim Yasuda, © 2002-04 JimCom
www.jimcom.net

Printed in Canada
Text printed on acid-free paper

Library of Congress Cataloging-in-Publication Data Pending

For

Nicholas and Henrietta Pearson

OTHER BOOKS BY TOM CHEETHAM

*The World Turned Inside Out: Henry Corbin and
Islamic Mysticism*
(2003)

*Green Man, Earth Angel: The Prophetic Tradition and
the Battle for the Soul of the World*
(2005)

Contents

The quotation on p. xiv is taken from Panayiotis Nellas, *Deification in Christ: Orthodox Perspectives on the Nature of the Human Person*, trans. Norman Russell (Crestwood, NY: St. Vladimir's Seminary Press, 1987), p. 16.

The quotation on p. 147 is taken from Tomas Tranströmer, "Out in the Open," trans. Robert Bly, in *Selected Poems: 1954-1986*, ed. Robert Hass (Hopewell, NJ: Ecco Press, 1987), p. 88.

Acknowledgments

The essays that make up this book would not have been written without the support and generosity of Nicholas Pearson and the members of the Temenos Academy in London, England. The labor of writing is solitary, and difficult at best. For several years, the Temenos Academy provided me with the opportunity to present my work to audiences who were encouraging, thoughtful, and sympathetic. Without the chance to share my thoughts in a community of friends, I would have no doubt remained mute.

I have a special place in my heart for Nick and Henrietta Pearson, who first bravely welcomed a stranger into their lives. My fondness for them is beyond words and my debt beyond all measure. We share bright memories of many feasts. This book is for them.

I owe a particular debt to David L. Miller of Syracuse University and the Pacifica Graduate Institute, whose kind, patient, and selfless help has made the book much better than it would otherwise have been. His support and encouragement have meant very much to me for several years.

Without the good-humored and efficient labors of Stephen Overy at the Temenos Academy there would have been no talks. The talk that became Chapter Five was written at the urging of John Carey who drew out thoughts that would otherwise have remained inarticulate. His meticulous scholarship has often saved me from embarrassment. I am deeply happy to have been the recipient of the hospitality and friendship of John, his wife, Stella von Boch, and their wonderful children, Lavinia and Francis, in whose company I spent many quiet and contented hours.

Nancy Cater of Spring Journal Books has been an invaluable help in a variety of usual and unusual circumstances over the last few years and I am exceedingly grateful for her encouragement and support.

As has been the case for many years now, I continue to rely on the interlibrary loan staff at the Bangor Public Library. Their efficient labors make this work possible and I do not know how I would manage without them.

My wife and children have endured and supported me during my long struggle with Henry Corbin and the realm of the imaginal. They are the heart and the soul of my world. Everything that matters most I have learned from them.

Versions of the following chapters have been presented as Temenos Academy Lectures in London: "The Un-Refused Feast," October 2004 (and published in *Spring: A Journal of Archetype and Culture 74— Alchemy*); "Mystical Poverty and the Theory of the World" and "The Flame of Things," September 2005 (a much different version of "Mystical Poverty" was presented at the 2001 Eranos Conference in Ascona, Switzerland under a different title and later appeared in the *Temenos Academy Review 9*); "The Cross of Light" and "Touching Grace" were presented in October, 2006, the latter being published in the *Temenos Academy Review 10*. Versions of parts of Chapter 6 were presented as a lecture for the Master's Program in the Cultural Study of Cosmology and Divination at The University of Kent, Canterbury, England, October, 2006.

Tom Cheetham
2007

Preface

This volume completes a trilogy of works in which the vision of Henry Corbin plays a central role. In the first, *The World Turned Inside Out: Henry Corbin and Islamic Mysticism* (2003), I tried to present an ac ount of his thought that would serve as an objective and sympathetic introduction for the general reader. In this, as in the second book, *Green Man, Earth Angel: The Prophetic Tradition and the Battle for the Soul of the World* (2005), I have been less concerned with presenting a balanced view of the details of his position, and more with how we might interpret and appropriate some of the powerful ideas that he presents. Corbin was a mystic, a philosopher, and a theologian of the first rank as well as a prodigious scholar of Islam—a figure whose breadth and depth of knowledge presents difficulties for many people who could benefit from the liberating spiritual guidance his work contains. I hope that I have neither oversimplified nor misrepresented his work. I like to think that I have made some of his central ideas more accessible than they would otherwise have been. The thoughts presented here are the fruit of my personal encounter with Corbin's vast intellectual endeavor. These essays are meditations which have his work as their primary inspiration. A wise friend of mine, hearing of my first book on Corbin, said, "I see that you have become the student of a student of Sufism." I am not sure that I can claim even that. I stand in awe of Corbin's scholarship, but I am not myself a scholar of anything in particular. Yet I have spent some time trying to make his work clear to myself, and I have been delighted that the results of the effort have been useful to others. His book on Ibn 'Arabi, *Creative Imagination in the Sufism of Ibn 'Arabi* (1969), remains, I think, the best introduction to his thought. It is a masterpiece of beauty and inspiration—an initiatory experience well within the capacity of any serious reader, and more worthwhile reading than anything that I have written.

There are several themes that together form what I take to be the core of the spirituality that Corbin defends. The Imagination plays a crucial role in the human and divine orders. It is the primary means by which we engage with Creation, and it provides the link "without which the worlds are put out of joint." Prayer is the supreme form of the creative imagination, and as such is the ultimate exercise of human freedom. Opposing the imagination is rigid literalism in its myriad forms. Corbin presents a vehement triple critique of idolatry, dogma, and the institutionalization of religion, coupled with a radical assessment of the doctrine of the Incarnation. He considered himself a Protestant Christian, but he abandoned the Christocentric view of history. The importance of the ecumenical approach he outlined cannot be overstated. The grand sweep of his theology of the Holy Spirit embraces Judaism, Christianity, and Islam as manifestations of a single coherent story of the ongoing relationship between the individual and God. He pleaded for recognition of the over-arching unity of the religions of Abraham. He was a passionate defender of the central role of the individual as the finite image of the Unique Divine. It is the bond between the human soul and the unique face of the Heavenly Twin, the Angel Holy Spirit, that is the ethical bond *par excellence*. This mystical spirituality depends upon the capacity of the human soul to travel a path towards the Angel, and towards perfection. The status of Person is not simply bestowed upon us at birth—it is a goal to be achieved. The true journey of our lives is measured on a vertical scale. Our progress on this path is gauged by our capacity for love and, linked to this, our ability to perceive beauty. One of the things that initially drew me to Corbin's work is his emphasis on the beauty and glory of natural world. His mystic vision sees all of Creation as a theophany of the divine. Beauty is the supreme theophany, and human love for a being of beauty is not a hindrance to our union with the Divine, but an entryway to Divine Passion. This vision has much in common with what has become known as Creation Spirituality, and the figure of the Angel Holy Spirit is similar to what is sometimes called the Cosmic Christ. If there is to be a future for the prophetic tradition that transcends mutual suspicion, hatred, and violence, it will be one in which Corbin's work can play an important role.

One person besides Corbin who figures prominently in these pages is Ivan Illich. I have long been in the disturbing position of being profoundly attracted by aspects of both their visions of Christianity. In most respects, their theologies, their styles, and their temperaments could not be more different. Reading them against each other has been a difficult and enlightening experience, and my understanding of some central theological questions has been deepened thereby. Illich provides a counterweight to certain aspects of Corbin's mysticism with which I have at times been uneasy. For all their differences, they share a deep distrust of institutional religion, and are passionate defenders of the dignity and freedom of the individual. They provide inspiring examples of how one might live a genuinely religious life on the margins of the institutional Church.

Fear a system, say the Fathers, as you would fear a lion.

—Panayiotis Nellas

CHAPTER ONE

Mystical Poverty and the Theory of the World

THE REFUSAL OF THE POETS

L isten to these excerpts from a haunting meditation, written by a young Henry Corbin in 1932 at the edge of Lake Siljan in Sweden. He called it *Theology by the Lakeside*:

> Everything is but revelation; there can only be re-velation. But revelation comes from the Spirit, and there is no knowledge of the Spirit.
>
> It will soon be dusk, but for now the clouds are still clear, the pines are not yet darkened, for the lake brightens them into transparency. And everything is green with a green richer than pulling all the organ stops in recital. It must be heard seated, very close to the Earth, arms crossed, eyes closed, pretending to sleep.
>
> For it is not necessary to strut about like a conqueror and want to give a name to things, to everything; it is they who will tell you who they are, if you listen, yielding like a lover; for suddenly for you, in the untroubled peace of this forest of the North, the Earth has come to Thee, visible as an Angel that would perhaps be a woman, and in this apparition, this greatly green and thronging solitude, yes, the Angel too is robed in green, the green of dusk, of silence and of truth. Then there is in you all the sweetness that is present in the surrender to an embrace that triumphs over you ....

> ... [A]t each moment where you read *in truth* as now what
> is there before you, where you hear the Angel, and the Earth
> and Woman, then you receive Everything, Everything, in your
> absolute poverty ....
>   ... [Y]ou are the poor one, you are man; and he is God,
> and you cannot know God, or the Angel, or the Earth, or
> Woman. You must be encountered, taken, known, that they
> may speak, otherwise you are alone ....[1]

We are the poor ones, and only in poverty can we hear these voices. But too many of us lust for power and do strut about like conquerors. And much of the energy of modern Western culture has been devoted to the attempt to gain dominion over creation. The quest for power always turns violent in the end, fundamentalisms spring up everywhere, and people find themselves in conflict with each other and with the creatures with whom we share the earth, deaf to any voices but their own.

In the so-called developed world, and increasingly everywhere, people live immersed in the frenzies and obsessions of commercial culture, amidst the products of extravagant and damaging tools, and assaulted by the powerful, exciting, and fragmenting images generated by global capitalism. It seems self-evident to many that such lives are the richest the world has ever known. And surely in some sense this is true. But in so far as we live in a world dominated by the products of the human economy, oriented towards producing and gratifying human desires, we will suffer from a dangerous restriction of experience, thought, and expression, and of our capacities for love and relationship, lacking even the memory of the desire for transcendence.

The vision that Corbin presents is of a wholly different form of life. To understand it we need to know what he means by poverty. It is not the desperate curse of the impoverished, but rather a voluntary attempt to live *unattached* and so freed from passions for control. At the heart of the search for poverty is the renunciation of power. This is radical, but every religious tradition has its examples.

Poverty is the fundamental condition of human existence. Corbin calls this metaphysical state *mystical* poverty: all things derive not from themselves, but from a source that is the grantor of Being to everything. Mystical poverty is the true state of all beings: each and every thing *has* nothing in itself, *is* nothing in itself. Corbin tells us of the 17th-century Shi'ite, Mir Damad, who heard "the great occult clamor of beings," the "silent clamor of their metaphysical distress"; it appeared to him as a music of cosmic anguish and as a sudden black light invading the cosmos.[2] This is a direct experience of what philosophers ca ͽ the contingency of being, and it gives rise to the great question of metaphysics: "Why is there something rather than nothing?" For the gnostic, it takes the form of a moment of annihilation and terror, destroying the solid foundations upon which the *ego* and the literal world are built. In Corbin's words,

> The black light reveals the very secret of being, which can only *be* as *made-to-be*; all beings have a twofold face, a face of light and a black face. The luminous face, the face of day, is the only one that … the common run of m⁄ perceive …. Their black face, the one the mystic perceives, is their poverty …. The totality of their being is their daylight face and their night face ….[3]

The wonder and terror in the face of the fact that there *is*, but only by the grace of God, something rather than nothing, provide the opening to the Unknown that lies at the heart of creation. To cover over this terrible wonderment is to block access to an Absence that is not the empty Nothing of nihilism, but the unknown and unknowable source of everything: the necessarily Hidden God beyond all being. We are owed nothing, because everything is gratuitous— it is all a Gift.

Corbin has explained that there are two sources of darkness. One is the darkness of evil, which actively refuses the Light of God. The other is the Darkness of the Black Light, which is the final perilous stage of the mystical journey. This is the darkness that Nietzsche misunderstood as the Void, and so announced the death of God. To understand poverty as the renunciation of both power and need, it is necessary to see how it is that the human *ego* is undone through the encounter with the Hidden God, who is the Breath that grants being to all things. Corbin writes:

> … [T]he initial principle from which the world derived, and which must explain it, must never be something contained in this world, and simultaneously it is necessary for this initial principle to possess all that is necessary to explain at once the being and the essence of the world and that which it contains …. It is necessary … that this initial principle be at once "all" and "nothing" …. [This] is a … nothing from which all things

are derived. This is the Nothing of the Absolute Divine, superior
to being and thought.[4]

This is the Black Face of the majesty of Divinity, the essential
counterweight to the Face of Light, the Face of Beauty of the revealed
cosmos. One cannot have the one without the other. Majesty without
Beauty is annihilation pure and simple. Beauty without Majesty would
be an unbearable Absolute frozen in eternal, changeless immanence—
a permanent, horrible, all-pervading Final Truth. All of Creation,
including, pre-eminently, the human person, is balanced between these
poles, constantly created, and constantly undone in the divine
interplay between transcendence and immanence, darkness and light,
Majesty and Beauty.

The Absolute beyond-being is also, in the Abrahamic tradition,
the Absolute Subject. The Giver of being can never be an object, a
thing. In its infinite fecundity and mystery, its forever-receding
depth and absolute Unity, it is the unifier, the guarantor of the
individuality of every being. As such, it is the archetype of the Person,
and of the interiority that infuses all the beings of the Earth
experienced as an Angel.

It is the mystery of this primordial Darkness that it establishes the
substantial reality of the human person and yet simultaneously renders
us transparent. We are made and unmade in every moment. And it lies
very close at hand. It is the still, small voice of the Hebrew Bible[5]; and
in the Qur'an God says "I am closer to you than your jugular vein."[6]
The presence of this pregnant darkness is immanent, shimmering
through the face of the beauty of the world. Feeling this eliminates a
certain kind of deep spiritual *neediness*. Scarcity and plenitude are
complementary, not contradictory. A degree of poverty is a prerequisite
for the experience of the fullness of the world. This poverty is the result
of letting go of a desperate grip upon the world. Creation unfolds only
when power is renounced. For the things of this world grow opaque when
we try to control and possess them. They withdraw into themselves and
block our access to the riches at the roots of things.

Many of our tools, perhaps now most of them, originate from a
hypertrophy of this neediness and these fears. As a result of our
technologies, the rich nations are consuming the resources of the earth
at a terrifying pace and the gap between the wealthy and the destitute
widens. Perhaps some small steps can be taken towards preventing the

domination of humanity by the tools we have created, and perhaps this could help prevent the social catastrophes that inevitably follow when the rich are able to ignore the suffering of the poor. We need to nurture *counter-technologies* not grounded in the desire for power, technologies that can help reveal that everything we need is already at hand. They cannot be based upon the assumptions of modern technology: that knowledge is synonymous with power, and power is always good, and that knowledge must invariably be exercised by changing the world.

I used to think that it is the kind of knowledge pursued by science and technology that sets constraints and limits on us, that tells us what we can and cannot do, that gets to the hard-nosed, rock-bottom *facts* of the world; and I used to think that poets and artists inhabited a realm of unconstrained freedom of imagination. Poets, on this view, are the ones who flee from the harsh realities of the real world revealed by Reason, into the happy lands of fantasy and imagination.

I was wrong. It is science and technology that refuse nothing. For the dogmatists of secular rationalism, Knowledge is Power. There is nothing in the universe that cannot be, that should not be, unveiled. Nothing is inviolate.

And what of the poets then? They are the refusers. It is they who set limits, who disclose concrete, particular, and personal worlds. They speak to us out of intimacy. They are the guardians of the inviolate individual, of the mystery of the Person.

Corbin tells us that a fundamental characteristic of the human person is to be *oriented* in a world. This orientation has nothing to do with public space or time, and is irreducibly personal. It is indeed the essence of what it means to be a person, and lacking any orientation whatsoever, we are lost as Corbin says "in vagabondage and perdition."[7] The public world can become a world *for us* only if it is transformed by what Corbin calls *interiorization*. This transformation occurs simultaneously to the world and to the soul. Or better, the human soul and the soul of the world are revealed as inextricably linked. A violation of either is a violation of both. The birth of the human person, and the revelation of the soul of the world are accomplished by a kind of "turning-inside-out" of each, giving the outer world the interiority of the personal soul and the inner person the confident reality of the outer world.

The knowledge offered by public reason will not provide orientation. However useful it may be, it provides only rules and the objects to which they apply. It is the poets who are the guardians of the person and of the soul of the world. Any counter-technology will be based on their work, and it can be founded on the ancient technologies of poverty, the virtues of refusal and renunciation, which are called *ascesis*. Asceticism is not the denial of joy and beauty, but their foundation. Asceticism is not a rejection of our capacity to be open to pleasure, love, and beauty, but a recognition of the limitations inherent in our finitude. We can love only what we can be intimate with, and intimacy is of necessity limiting, immediate, and personal. It is, in traditional language, *chaste*. *Chastity* is the refusal of the exteriorization of the soul; it is a refusal to become fragmented, disoriented, disembodied, and violated by the passions to which our neediness makes us prey. Neediness is the opposite of freedom and is a form of idolatry: what it idolizes are things, or people regarded as things; and things never suffice. The human economy depends upon this idolatrous relation and the calculus of values that it requires. Poverty makes it possible to receive the gift of intimacy and friendship that comes from a Person. Intimacy allows the recognition of what is finally the ultimate Good for each of us, which can only be another person. What else could it be?[8]

───────────

And so I turn to poetry and the imagination in the quest for that form of life which Henry Corbin reveals in his meditation by the lake. It is in part a question of *aesthetics*. There are deep connections between *ascesis* and *aesthesis*, between conscious and careful renunciation and attention to the beauty and animation of the world. Each requires discrimination based on careful feeling. It is possible at least, and first of all, to refuse to become unconsciously ensnared by the allurements of a commercialized world. It is so easy to become overwhelmed and numbed by the impact of too many things, too many ideas, too many images, all of which are the work of someone somewhere else, for purposes not our own, and none of which are the result of our own making, our own transformations of the world. To begin to be sensitive to the manifold effects of this impersonal world on our actions, thoughts, and emotions and so gain some distance from it is already an act of renunciation and of aesthetic discrimination.

The attention required to perceive the beauty and interiority of the world opens us to the realm that Corbin calls the *mundus imaginalis*, the *imaginal* world. The imagination is the supreme function of the human heart. Perception of the beauty and interiority of the world and of other people requires a break-down of the barrier between ideas and emotions experienced as private and internal and things "out there" in the public world. What C. G. Jung called the *feeling function* must be active, because it is feeling, in his sense of the term, that provides the connection between the inner and the outer. Even seemingly abstract ideas "in our heads" and things "out there" are not always clearly distinguishable. Indeed this is evident from the practice of science. The most abstruse ideas of theoretical physics transform all too readily into concrete things such as thermonuclear warheads. Corbin and Jung have taught us that there is no clear division between the physical and the psychic. There is a kind of thought that is not directed towards the manipulation and control of objects, which opens onto the realm of the *imaginal*, that mediating world where thoughts are embodied and bodies are spiritualized. Jung speaks of the "thing-like-ness of thought,"[9] and Corbin says, "... [U]ltimately what we call *physis* and the physical is but the reflection of the world of the Soul; there is no pure physics, but always the physics of some definite psychic activity."[10] The realm of subtle bodies and of embodied thoughts seems to a rationalist consciousness only confusion and nonsense. But it is the modern abstract world of public, objective things that is *an-aesthetic* and non-sensical, and wholly incapable of supporting the presence of persons.

Right at the roots of the Western philosophical tradition there is a striking contrast with the dominant modern conception of the nature of thinking. For instance, Aristotle assumed a kind of relation between thought and things, a notion that is nearly incomprehensible to the modern mind. He writes that "the soul is somehow all beings."[11] And Plotinus: "When we know (the intelligibles) we do not have images or impressions of them ... but we are them."[12] This kind of knowledge was experienced as a *conjunction* between the knower and the known. Such intercourse is intensely and actively imaginative and depends upon highly developed and articulate feeling.

Plotinus tells us that access to this experience requires an annihilating encounter with the Hidden God, an experience akin to the vision of the Black Light described by Corbin. Access to this

boundary-breaking experience requires a special kind of in-sight, which
Plotinus calls *theoria*. This seeing, or *theasthai*, requires the ability to
"let go of being" in a moment of nothingness. Such letting go results
in wonderment, *thauma*, and the transformation of discursive reason
into an open-ended process that makes possible the continual undoing
of definitive, dogmatic statements and perceptions.[13] The Greek *thauma*
means "a wonder, a thing compelling to the gaze."[14] The gaze that is
turned upon this wonder is the *theoria*, an interiorizing contemplation
of the theophanic apparition. Here again, thought and thing are not
disjunct: the word *thauma* is the source of both *theory* and *theater*, both
speculation and spectacle, seeing with the mind and seeing with the
eye. John Deck, in a study of Plotinus, writes, "'*Theoria,*' with its
cognate verb, qeorein, seems to have evolved in meaning from 'sending
an official see-er to the games,' to 'being a spectator at the games,' to
'being a spectator generally,' (i.e., simply 'seeing, viewing'), to
'contemplating, contemplation.'"[15] What I want to suggest is that
while for us "theoretical" means abstract, logical, formal, and even
connotes irrelevance, it has its origins in an experience of the world
that was wondrous, concrete, sensuous, and imaginative. This is the
kind of aesthetics and the kind of imagination that concern us here.

THE THEORY OF THE WORLD

Harmony & Synaesthesia

In Islamic thought, the world of Nature is the Primordial
Revelation, open to all who have eyes to see, as the original Creation
in which the signs of God are written. God breathes this world into
being. In his great book on Ibn 'Arabi, Corbin tells us that the act of
creation was not a violent drama of power and omnipotence. Rather,
God says: "I was a Hidden Treasure and I yearned to be known. Then
I created creatures in order to be known by them." This divine passion
born of loneliness is the motive for the Creation. The unrevealed God
experienced anguish in the darkness of his occultation, and, Corbin
tells us,

> ... from the inscrutable depths of the Godhead this sadness calls
> for a "Sigh of Compassion." This Sigh marks the release of the
> divine Sadness sym-pathizing with the anguish and sadness of
> His divine names that have remained unknown, and in this very

> act of release the Breath exhales, arouses to active being, the
> multitude of individual concrete existences by and for which
> these divine names are at last actively manifested.[16]

But the Breath of God is also His Word And so the whole of Creation
is a sort of Book, an embodiment of the Word, manifesting the Names
of God. No wonder, then, that the particular Revelation to the people
of Islam should be in fact a literal Book, the Qur'an. In this vision,
the world and all its creatures are perceived as sensible signs, parts of
a vast language embodying the Speech, and indeed the Song, of
Creation. Here Speech and Song are the original, originating creative
acts. Speech and Song are the primordial technologies of the world.

   The perception of *harmony* is one of the most fundamental features
of the cosmos that Corbin describes for us. It is a harmony that is not
only literally musical. The imaginal realm is the proper home of
aesthesis, and this primary aesthetics is grounded in a cosmological
synaesthesia. The exercise of Imagination gives substance to a subtle
body in which all the five senses are fused to "constitute a single
synaesthesis."[17] Not only do *thought* and *thing* fuse, but all our senses,
and all the things we sense are linked by the resonances and the
harmonies among them. The knowledge that the Sufis seek reveals itself
as a kind of *taste* (*dhawq*). And recall Corbin's vision of an Earth in
which "everything is green with a green richer than pulling all the organ
stops in recital." There is a sophisticated treatment of this theme in
the work of Maurice Merleau-Ponty. He argues that such synaesthetic
experience lies at the heart of the "animistic consciousness" that is the
preconceptual foundation of all our perceptions.[18] For both Corbin
the   mystic   theologian   and   Merleau-Ponty   the   secular
phenomenologist, the recovery of the *anima mundi* is a return to a
lost realm that is perhaps hidden, but is always at hand. This mode of
perception may in some sense be mystical, but it pulls us deeply *into*
the world that we share with the creatures around us, not out of it.
All the beings of the world are connected within and among themselves
by the vibrations of harmonic *sympathy*. Our place among them is not
one of dominion, but of interconnection. All beings share a common
desire to orient themselves towards their proper origin and sing the
songs that are the music of their world. Even the flowers. Corbin cites
passages from the 5th-century Neoplatonist, Proclus, in which he
describes the movements of the *Heliotrope* as it keeps its face turned

towards the sun. Proclus writes, "... [E]ach thing prays according to
the rank it occupies in nature ...; for the heliotrope ... [produces] a
hymn to its king such as it is within the power of a plant to sing."[19]
This harmonic perception is not a flight from reality into some
immaterial realm of abstraction. It requires deep immersion into the
common world of creatures. The 13th-century Anatolian Sufi, Da'ud
Qaysari, writes: "... [A]nimals *see* things which, among human beings,
can be seen only by the visionary mystics."[20]

Because of the harmonic structure of the world, there is indeed
something special about music and about speech as the music of the
word. It is music that most readily expresses the experience of a
synaesthetic space-time in which the Word speaks the forms of beings
in the spaces of the heart. Corbin writes:

> Th[e] homologation of forms in time with forms in space offers
> a particularly subtle case of *isomorphism*. It is this, in reality, which
> leads us to conceive of *many modes of spatiality*, among which
> the visual mode, corresponding to sensible perception, is not
> perhaps even the privileged case. Speech, the Divine Word ...
> is the sonorous incantation which evokes beings and which
> remains the profound and secret nature of each being. ... [T]his
> nature does not reveal itself, however, to the empirical point of
> view, but to another visual sense, to an *interior vision* perceiving
> other spaces. But precisely these spaces, and this psycho-spiritual
> spatiality, which has other properties than sensible space, require
> in their turn a homologation of sonorous space to supersensible
> spaces where the vibrations of the Word propagate as "arpeggios
> charged by distant lights."[21]

Words and music have the capacity to express similar harmonic
structures, that is to say, they are *isomorphic*. Prayer and poetry are
forms of music and *vice versa*. Corbin says that the "theophanic method
of discourse" recommended as a means of prayer by Ibn 'Arabi is
perhaps itself "nothing other than a form ... of the *progressio
harmonica*," and that "[s]omething in the nature of harmonic
perception is needed in order to perceive a world of many
dimensions."[22] Because of the synaesthetic nature of the imagination,
the reverberations of the Word can correspond both to the Images
which gather themselves in the spectacle of the *theoria,* and to the
repetitions of a melody in ascending octaves. Each repetition of a form
both preserves and alters that form, the form of a person, a situation,

an event, but each time at a different level of being. It is the Imagination that is the mirror, the *locus* for the spectacle, and so gives access to the reality of the sonorous spaces in which the being of things reverberates.

I am no mystic, as Corbin evidently was, and have no special access to exalted states, though I do not doubt their reality. But I am quite sure that everyone has some degree of access to these realities and can learn to move in these spaces, and that doing so makes transformation possible.

The harmonic structure of the world explains the possibility of spiritual transformation. When harmonic sympathy is fully in operation, then *to speak* is *to be*. Understanding something, we say we can *make sense* of it, and now it is clear that this making sense is not theoretical, but is primarily aesthetic, concrete, and sensuous. At root, it is the result of the active imagination both perceiving and establishing harmonies between the self and the world. Because of the harmonies that constitute the being of the things in creation, each individual can *make sense* only of what he or she *is*. What I can experience is a reflection of my being. I can be in sympathy only with those parts of creation with which I am in resonance. Thus, my life in its entirety is a measure of what I know. This is the basic principle of alchemy as well, that like can be known only by like. The form of understanding that Corbin describes in his work (he uses the technical term *hermeneutics* for this) is an alchemical, transformational process of coming to consciousness—consciousness not only of my own soul, but that of the world as well.

Notice that *hermeneutics* as a theological and philosophical term refers to the interpretation of a *text*. All understanding is in the broadest sense a phenomenon of Language. Thus the centrality of "poetry."

And this coming to consciousness is far from the development of an *ego* that would devour the world—it is a surrender. Again, recall Corbin's passion: "You must be encountered, taken, known, that they may speak ...." Rilke writes of someone in a similar encounter:

> Winning does not tempt that man.
> This is how he grows: by being defeated, decisively,
> by constantly greater beings.[23]

When imagination and renunciation are wed, then all the world becomes sensuous and my individual world, my life, can make sense to me. The spiritual world is no longer abstract and distant, but alive and intensely real. The true meaning of the word *substance* has faded from our consciousness. The spirit *is* substantial. Understanding this can help reclaim a sense of the concrete significance of the individual. The real work is simultaneously a spiritual, ethical, and physical struggle. Like can be known only by like—this means that thought and being are inseparable, that ethics and perception are complementary. The form of my soul is the form of my world. The fundamental unity of the faculties of cognition and the world to which they give access *is* the synaesthetic substrate for of all perception. A world becomes *real* and original insofar as it is the dwelling place of an individual person.

To grasp the significance of language for spiritual development, it is useful to consider the experience of the embodiment of the Word in Islamic spirituality. The Qur'an is first and foremost a *recited* text. Dr. Hossein Nasr writes:

> The whole experience of the Qur'an for Muslims remains to this day first of all an auditory experience and is only later associated with reading in the ordinary sense of the word. There is an ever-present, orally heard, and memorized Qur'an in addition to the written version of the Sacred Text, an auditory reality which touches the deepest chords in the souls of the faithful, even if they are unable to read the Arabic text.[24]

The power of the word, its poetic, musical force, is based upon vocalization, not silent, private reading. The Revelation of the Qur'an to Mohammad occurred as *recitation*, and the revelations, which continued throughout his life, were physically overwhelming. Islamic spirituality has retained this emphasis on embodiment throughout its history. The very position of the ritual prayer is said to have provided the archetype for the design of the human body. Prayer and its orientation towards Mecca as the symbol of centrality celebrate the worshipping body.[25]

And there is no clear distinction between the sacred and the secular in Islam. There cannot be a merely utilitarian realm, in which secular technology can get a foothold. There is no realm of life that is outside the religion. The Prophet Mohammad is seen as an exemplar of the perfect human, something that some Christians find difficult to understand, raised as they have been with a spiritualized image of

Christ as the archetype of holiness. Mohammad was a husband and father many times over, confidant, warrior, teacher, politician, businessman, prophet, and mystic: the fullness of human worldliness *and* spirituality, the perfection of that breathing body and microcosm of the world which is the human self. He provides a model for the substantial struggle of human life, for *gnosis* as the transformational knowledge that alters the networks of connections linking the microcosm and the macrocosm.

The phenomenology of the imaginal is central to the physicality of Islamic spirituality. William Chittick puts it quite clearly: "Imagination embodies. It cannot conceive of God or anything else save in concrete terms."[26] It is characteristic of Qur'anic Arabic that it is concrete: "... [T]he Arabic of the Qur'an ... always has a concrete side to it, and this is true of Arabic in general ...."[27]

On Ibn 'Arabi's view, both reason and imagination are required for adequate knowledge of the self, the world, and God. Certainly, in the absence of reason, we can be misled into delusion. Yet reason alone is dangerously one-sided. The imagination prevents the rupture between matter and spirit that is characteristic of our tradition. Chittick says:

> ... [I]magination perceives that the symbol is identical with what it symbolizes, creation is the same as the Creator, the form is none other than the meaning, the body is the spirit, the locus of manifestation is nothing but God as manifest, and the image is the object. This perception ... is unmediated by any rational process—it is a tasting, an unveiling, a witnessing, an insight .... It is best exemplified in human experience precisely by concrete experience—tasting food, being carried away by music, falling in love. Theologically, imagination ... achieves an incontrovertible understanding that the creature is God ....
>
> The mysteries of the universe do not lie primarily in the universal laws and principles, even though these are mysterious enough. What is most mysterious and miraculous about the universe is its concrete particularity, its every object and inhabitant, each of which is ultimately unfathomable.[28]

For Ibn 'Arabi, language, imagination and the material realities of Creation are linked together through the flow of the Breath of the

Merciful. Perhaps, by recognizing the vitality and power of this worldview, it is possible to recover a sense of the meaningful substance of the work of human life. Perhaps we can, as Corbin did, learn from the way Islam safeguards the primordial unity of self and world in a sensuous, imaginative sympathy.

Reading Uncurled

We can begin by taking language very seriously. We can acknowledge its ability to transform the soul and the world. To speak a language based on sympathetic harmonies would protect against the dangers of abstraction and the dogmas that accompany it. Such a poetics could help us to live in what Corbin called a realized eschatology, that is, one that occurs *right now*.

Language can serve to open us to this intimate, personal communion. The search for such a language and the form of life that it requires is a quest to be open to the world without the fear of violation. Such a life presumes our fundamental mystical poverty, and thus avoids neediness, and it honors intimacy and chastity as indispensable for our orientation towards transcendence.

Language can function as a tool of the imagination, giving access to the synaesthetic experience that opens onto the tastes and textures of the world as the Manifestation of the Real. And the breath of our words and the rhythms of our speech are essential because they reflect the images that are inherent in the things of creation.

A language is concrete in the sense that Chittick describes when its words are pregnant with images. Poetic language can be concrete in this way. Image opens onto image, landscape onto landscape, stitching the inner and outer together and enacting the sympathies between beings by means of perceptions of the subtle relations that link all things. This requires a kind of attention and perceptual skills that have atrophied in us from lack of use.

Those of us who live in a world of real abstractions have seen that the result of abstract thought, theoretical in the modern sense, can be the construction of a world that exhibits little sympathy for human or any other beings. Knowing the inhumanities and excesses of a world so designed, we can turn to the more difficult task of transformation that the thing-like-ness of concrete thought implies. We can turn to the real work of being human.

So many of us live too much within a world of our own making, immersed in degraded and increasingly meaningless forms of human language. We need open, challenging, and creative uses of language, an understanding of reading as a spiritual activity, and the conception of the person that this entails. We in the West are heirs to a dominant, and fundamentally masculine, tradition in which the self is understood and experienced as isolated and insecure: in Luther's words, *incurvare in se*, curved in upon itself.[29] Insofar as we have succumbed to this tradition, we have to learn to read and speak ourselves out of ourselves, and uncurl ourselves back into the world. Language is not only a tool for communication, manipulation, and advertising, nor does it belong only to us. It is not an exclusively human ability at all, but a field of energies and intentions that we inhabit. We speak because the world speaks. And because language and the symbols upon which it depends are the Breath of God, it has the power to penetrate to the very heart of things. Language in the broadest sense is creative because the world was spoken, breathed, sung into being. Because of this, reading, when rightly understood, *can* be, in the words of Ivan Illich, "an ontologically remedial technique,"[30] a means of transformation. David Abram has convincingly argued that the reading of a written text is a special, highly focused instance of the primary animism that pervades all perception, and that in literate cultures the animate participation between the self and the natural world has all but disappeared as our reliance on human language as the sole vehicle of meaning has become nearly total.[31] We need to learn to read other texts, and in other ways.

It seems clear that in many segments of modern society the habits and skills of literate culture are in fact being lost, but they are being replaced by an immersion of the soul in technological gadgetry and media-controlled capitalism, which only exacerbates our isolation from nature and from other persons. Technological societies may indeed be entering a time that George Steiner calls the After-word. The habits of reading and the culture of the book are on the decline. Both Steiner and Illich have somewhat wistfully proposed that perhaps as the universities turn themselves into the handmaidens of business, technology, and the military, we may yet preserve cells of resistance, "Houses of Reading" where the habits of mind of a bookish civilization can endure. I believe with them that something like this is essential for the preservation of our humanity, essential if we are to take a stand against the ongoing violations that are the annihilation of the person and the rape of nature. But this should not be a retreat into merely human language. It is possible to expand the imagination of reading, and of meaning. The cosmos itself is a "house of reading"—it is the Primordial Temple of the Word. Many of the guardians of high culture, of literature and the humanities, have for a long time not read this book at all. And when it is read, as it is by natural scientists, it is too often only in the most abstract languages of domination and control. The cultures of the After-word will not just be illiterate, but also denatured, dysfunctional, and condemned to occupy a world made in the human image and by human hands.

What are the techniques necessary to hear the voices of the persons who call to us? We know that a kind of *ascesis* is required, one that can lead to the perception of the black light at the heart of things, to our mystical poverty, and the renunciation of power. To open ourselves to the voices beyond the human requires as well a poet's attentiveness, and this requires some disciplines that are sorely lacking. Perhaps "houses of reading" are necessary to serve as cells of resistance to the domination of those who control the post-literate culture of the wholly un-natural. But these would be half-open dwellings, opening outward beyond the confines of the *ego*, to the persons of other cultures and beyond the range of human culture onto the mysteries of the more-than-human world. The harmonic structure of the world is such that we can hear the cries of other humans better when we can hear the voices of the more-than-human others as well.

Reading the world can take the form of a dialogue that begins with a careful listening to the voices that speak from beyond the bounds of the known. We can learn to be sensitive across the range of our sensory and emotional registers to the resonances, the hidden connections among all the sensuous displays of the world. Aspects of this kind of discipline can be learned from children, from certain kinds of natural and social science, and from poets and artists. George Steiner's profound study of the grounds of meaning in language is important here. We need a theory, that is, a *practice,* a *theoria*, not just of meaning in poetry and literature, but in the perception of all reality, and Steiner's suggestions are fertile. He recalls to us again the roots of the word *theoria*. "It tells," he writes,

> of concentrated insight, of an act of contemplation focused patiently on its object. But it pertains also to the deeds of witness

performed by the legates sent, in solemn embassy, to observe
the oracles spoken or the rites performed at the sacred Attic
games. A "theorist" or "theoretician" is one who is disciplined in
observance, a term itself charged with a twofold significance of
intellectual-sensory perception and religious or ritual conduct.
… Thus theory is inhabited by truth when it contemplates its
object unwaveringly and when, in the observant process of such
contemplation, it beholds, it takes grasp of the often confused
and contingent … images, associations, suggestions, possibly
erroneous, to which the object gives rise.[32]

This kind of attention is intensely real because it engages the natural
imagination of the body. The engagement with intelligible form as
presented in art requires that the work be experienced as a real
presence, and in this encounter the "poem, the statue, the sonata are
not so much read, viewed or heard as they are lived."[33] This is one
aspect of the harmonic perception Corbin explains to us. Art thus
"makes sense" of the world. But *aesthesis* refers to the perception of the
world we have not made, as much as of the world that we have. Steiner
understands that the perception of any meaningful form is grounded
in the encounter with a transcendence beyond the human. The
perception of *animation*, perhaps even of *reality* in art and in the world
is based upon what he calls the "axiom of dialogue."[34] We are always,
when we are truly paying attention, in communion with what lies
beyond us. Such communion presupposes the real presences that
populate the world. The flowers, the animals, the people, all the
persons of the earth. Steiner writes, "… [I]t is, I believe, poetry, art
and music which relate us most directly to that in being which is not
ours."[35] So, for George Steiner, one of the great theorists of the
imagination in our time, literature, art, and music are forms of dialogue
with the divine. Placed in the context of the harmonic theology that
Corbin displays for us, the consequences are breathtaking. For Corbin,
the creative imagination is the motive force for the liturgical structure
of the cosmos.

It is through the Creative Imagination that we participate in the
manifestations of the Divine. There are no autonomous "things," but
only manifestations of the Breath of Allah, bound together in the great
community of beings. When the mystic knows this, he realizes himself
to be the place where God knows Himself through His creation. The
Creative Imagination through which we perceive the harmonic

structure of reality, and which is the source of all true *theory*, is therefore
the sole means by which the world is known. This sensuous, sympathic,
and participatory knowledge of Creation reaches its peak of intensity
in prayer. All of creation participates in this prayer. As Proclus has told
us, "… [E]ach thing prays according to the rank it occupies in
nature."[36] In the scheme of celestial hierarchies presented by Qazi Sa'id
Qommi, a 17th-century Iranian Shi'ite, each Angelic hierarchy
celebrates a perpetual liturgy that transmits life and light to the level
below, and in turn the lower levels sing upwards and engage in hymns
of praise, each of which "plants a tree in Paradise."[37]

The entire cosmos is permeated by liturgies of creation and hymns
of praise. The whole of reality is meant to be one vast Prayer. Far from
being a plea sent towards a distant God, prayer is the means by which
Creator and Creature are irrevocably entwined, one with the other, in
mutual sympathy. For Corbin, "prayer is not a request for something:
it is the expression of a mode of being, a means of existing and of *causing
to exist* …."[38] It is the archetypal Creative Act. The deep structure of
the cosmos is a dynamic and creative activity that is liturgical and
doxological, and it is through rituals of prayer and praise *and* through
the practice of the arts conceived as such, that we most adequately
participate in the divine dynamism of things. Corbin says that through
the liturgical action of prayer "[w]e witness and participate in an entire
ceremonial of meditation, a psalmody in two alternating voices, one
human, the other divine …."[39] And so it is that we may read the
harmonies of the world, transforming ourselves as we do.

Henry Corbin should have the last words, there at the edge of the
lake where he saw a vision of the Angel of the Earth:

> … [A]t each moment where you read *in truth* as now what is
> there before you, where you hear the Angel, and the Earth and
> Woman, then you receive Everything, Everything, in your
> absolute poverty.
> … [Y]ou are the poor one, you are man; and he is God,
> and you cannot know God, or the Angel, or the Earth, or
> Woman. You must be encountered, taken, known, that they
> may speak, otherwise you are alone ….

CHAPTER TWO

The Un-Refused Feast

THE LOST SPEECH

In his late writings, Henry Corbin articulated particularly clearly his vision of the unity of the religions of Abraham.[1] This harmony depends upon a shared story centered on the revelation of the Word of God. Corbin writes:

> The drama common to all the "religions of the Book" ... can be designated as the drama of the "Lost Speech." And this because the whole meaning of their life revolves around the phenomenon of the revealed holy Book, around the true meaning of this Book. If the true meaning of the Book is the interior meaning, hidden under the literal appearance, then from the instant that men fail to recognize or refuse this interior meaning, from that instant they mutilate the unity of the Word, of the Logos, and begin the drama of the "Lost Speech."[2]

For Corbin, much of Judaic, Christian, and Islamic history can be understood only if it is seen as the theater in which the drama of the conflict between the literal and the hidden meanings of the Word is played out. To the degree that the Word is perceived only literally, to that degree is its true meaning lost.

For Corbin and the mystical theologians for whom he speaks, human language is a dim reflection of a spiritual world of poetic images that are at once sensuous and intellectual. The language of the angels is the language of the creative imagination. The language of poetry is as close as we can get to this divine imaginal speech, in which lies the interior meaning of the Word. Corbin's account of Western history traces the progressive loss of the Breath of Compassion, which speaks this language and so gives life and soul to the world. The loss of the realm of the *imaginal* inhabited by the Angel of Humanity and the Angel of the Earth occasioned all the schisms that split the West: religion and philosophy, thought and being, intellect and ethics, body and spirit, God and the individual. In this history, the place of language and the revealed Word is central, and the quest for the lost language of the angels is the fundamental task. It is *the* drama that underlies the unity of the three branches of the Abrahamic tradition.

––––––––––

Islam, as the last in the sequence of great Revelations in the Abrahamic tradition, sees itself as the culmination of the present cycle of prophecy. It is, as Martin Lings has put it, "something of a summation," and we might expect that the Qur'an would provide some guidance in our search for the lost language. Henry Corbin and Louis Massignon regarded what they take to be the central episode of Sura XVIII of the Qur'an as pivotal for understanding the Prophetic Tradition.[3] This is the story of the meeting between Moses and Khidr. Khidr is a mysterious figure who acts as Moses' spiritual Guide and initiator into the mystical truths, which Corbin says, "emancipate one from literal religion." It is this Guide who explains the inner and most personal meaning of the Law to Moses. Massignon has translated his name as "The Verdant One." He is the Green Man of Islamic tradition. Corbin tells us that he is associated with every aspect of nature's greenness. He has attained the source of Life and has drunk the water of immortality, and so is the Eternal Youth. He is the archetypal hermeneut, whose speech is the lost poetry of Creation. In the Islamic tradition, he is linked, and at times identified, with the Old Testament figure of Elijah. Khidr is the archetypal figure of the personal spiritual Guide, and Corbin says, equivalent to the Paraclete of the Gospel of John, the Hidden Imam of Shi'ism, and the Christ of the Cross of Light; he is the *True Prophet*, the inner guide of each person, the Angel Holy Spirit, whose appearance to every person is *for each one unique.*

The question posed by Islam, at the end of the prophetic tradition, after Moses, Jesus, and Mohammad, is: What comes after the Prophets? The central questions of Corbin's book on Ibn 'Arabi are: *Who is Khidr?* and *What does it mean to be a disciple of Khidr?*[4] This celestial person, common to all the religions of the Book, is the key to solving the mystery of the Lost Speech.

The inability, or the refusal, to hear the voice of the Verdant One and so recognize the inner meaning of the Word severs the link between the human person and the reality of the Imagination. By depriving us of the connection between language and divinity, this incapacity renders us deaf, dumb, blind, and lame. In this condition, we are so profoundly isolated that all our interactions with the world and the persons who inhabit it are hindered by ignorance, lack of sympathy, and the disoriented gropings that arise from a dim, inarticulate desire to restore the lost connection.

The withering of a primordial "poetic" sympathy is an archetypal phenomenon—it is an ever-present possibility inherent in the human condition. The loss marks the beginning of our exile. The drama of the Lost Speech is the story of the quest to return. All of us, at every moment, are balanced between the forces that would silence the inner voices of that forgotten language and the energies that would return us home to a world we dimly recall, and sometimes sense as a longing, the vague fragment of a song, or the memory of a Voice that calls our deepest, most secret Name.

This lost language of Eden is the speech of the Divine Person, of the Angel of Humanity, who is unique for each of us. This polymorphic celestial figure guarantees the personal reality of the world. The English language is a bit awkward here. It is a question of what might be called the "Person-hood" of the world, but that seems a bit stilted. Or perhaps we could say the "Person-ality" of the world, but that has the wrong connotations. I tend to favor the term *interiority*, but that misses the underlying theological resonance. However we speak of it, this imaginative reality that is the inner face of things is the source of the personification of the world. To the degree that the language of the imagination is lost, to that degree are people and all the elements of Creation de-personalized, turned into objects, into abstractions. The final result is Hell. The final result is a world without a Face.

Everything has a physiognomy: trees and flowers, all animals, buildings and landscapes, chairs, tables …. As Corbin asks, "… [W]hat would a world without face or features—without, that is to say, a look— actually be?"[5] All of reality shares something of the interiority of the Divine Person. For anything to *be* at all, it must fall within the power of this Person. But as our ability to perceive this interiority declines, the richness, variety, and complexity of our experience is compromised, our sympathy for the elements of creation withers, our desire to engage in dialogue wanes, and we end up with such limited means for interacting with the world and its inhabitants that all we can do is push them around aimlessly in frustration and anger.

The rationalist account of reality holds that we know about a thing or a person to the degree that we can describe and explain it. This may be true, in Hell. In Hell there are no persons, only objects. But in the approach to Eden, as we learn to discern the inner meaning of the Word and of the World, the more Real, the more *personal*, the beings of Creation become, the more *indescribable* they become. The poetic sensibility always leads towards that which cannot be spoken, yet which is most Real. The final, paradoxical, stage in the drama of the Lost Speech is to attain the freedom of the true Person and to speak a language whose end can only be the silence of contemplation.

To be a disciple of Khidr is to seek for the Speech within the interiority of the World. It requires that we live guided by the Imagination, seeking the primordial poetic sensibility that is necessary to experience the world in all its fullness and complexity. I think D. H. Lawrence's comment on the artistic life is pertinent for all of us: "I always feel as if I stood naked for the fire of Almighty God to go through me—and it's rather an awful feeling. One has to be so terribly religious to be an artist."[6]

But for the most part, those of us who live in a consumer society don't live by the interior imagination. We abdicate that responsibility and leave it to others to fill our heads with images and ideas. It is so easy to abandon ourselves to exteriority and disorientation, and so to be knocked about by our emotions and the manipulations of others, clinging to whatever transient stability is to be found in the public world. To wholly abandon the search for the interiority of the Lost Speech is to live a life governed by the multitudinous forms of *idolatry*. Corbin has defined both idolatry and its opposite for us:

> Idolatry consists in immobilizing oneself before an idol because
> one sees it as opaque, because one is incapable of discerning in
> it the hidden invitation that it offers to go beyond it. Hence,
> the opposite of idolatry would not consist in breaking idols, in
> practicing a fierce iconoclasm aimed against every inner or external
> Image; it would rather consist in rendering the idol transparent
> to the light invested in it. In short, it means transmuting the
> idol into an icon.[7]

This is one way of understanding the function of the Lost Speech: to render the world itself transparent, to reveal the iconic status of Creation. To be a disciple of Khidr is to apprentice oneself in the craft of the transmutation of idols into icons. Transmutation is, of course, an alchemical operation, and alchemical symbolism has the great virtue of combining the material and the spiritual in a dynamic tension which is imaginative and creative to the core. It is one of the central hidden themes of the Abrahamic tradition, and it has, as we shall see, a special relevance to Christianity.

PEACOCK'S FLESH AND THE BLOOD OF THE LION

The New Testament parable of the Feast is a story told by both Matthew and Luke. In Chapter 14 of the Gospel of Luke, Christ says, "A man once gave a great banquet, and invited many; and at the time for the banquet he sent his servant to say to those who had been invited, 'Come, for all is now ready.' But they all alike began to make excuses."[8] Being refused by the invited guests, who all have something better to do, the man sends his servants to the city streets to bring in "the poor and maimed and blind and lame," those, that is, who have nothing, and who do not refuse. Of this tale Corbin writes, "The Gospel Parable of the Feast means precisely what it says. ... It would be ridiculous to engage in polemics against men or women who refuse to come to the Feast; their refusal inspires only sadness and compassion."[9]

It is the refusal of the symbolic life, of the imagination, to which Corbin refers. The life to which he calls us implies a radically traditional metaphysics, which he spent his life articulating and defending. The compassion he feels is for those who refuse to admit the reality of a cosmos in which it is possible to be transformed, a cosmos in which what you can experience is a measure of who you are. The objectively real world to which the Imagination gives access, which Corbin called the *mundus imaginalis*, is embedded within an infinite creation, which has a vertical dimension: there is a kind of hierarchy of levels of being from the less real to the more real. Human beings can, by their actions and passions, become more real, more themselves, more individual; or they can "fall" and lose themselves in disorientation and confusion. If we think of this hierarchy as a Ladder or Chain of Being, we are likely to miss the point. Those who count themselves "post-modern" are very rightly suspicious of hierarchic power structures, but this is not a power structure. It has been so misconstrued with great regularity, but it is perhaps better to think of it as a liberating architecture, one that opens the soul and releases the powers of sympathy and compassion. When the lower soul, the *ego*, drops away, even if only for a moment—and this is often the best we can manage—we can see more clearly the beauty and the unselfish, giving love that connects us to the world and links all beings together. The hierarchy is ascended not so much by going "up," as one does in social hierarchies. In this movement of the soul, the motion is inwards, or better, outwards, but in a new way. We become more intensely real ourselves and so experience the world as more intensely real, more alive, more pregnant with lives and energies. The invitation to the plenitude of being is our birthright. We have been invited to the Feast, but so many find it so hard to hear that invitation, or to believe such revelry exists.

Why? Corbin's answer to this obvious question is also very traditional: Idolatry. We are all idolators. One reason for this is that being human is the most difficult task there is. Even a privileged life is full of confusion, pain, and suffering, and the lives of many are marked by measureless agonies. Sympathy calls us to compassionate action. Sympathy calls us into the world. But the world is complicated in ways we can only dimly comprehend, and the best intentions cannot guarantee the consequences of our acts. It is so easy to become confused, disheartened, angry, and despairing, to feel abandoned, exiled, and homeless. It is easy to lose faith, to become at best an agnostic, at worst, a nihilist—and so then to *become* the poor, the maimed, the blind, and the lame. Such souls are isolated and confused, and cling in desperation to whatever idols promise simple, clear, stable answers to the intractable problems of life. But it is the painful state of poverty and abandonment that is the first step on the path of Return. Remember that in the same chapter of the Gospel of Luke, Christ, stunningly, says: "... [W]hoever of you does not renounce all that he has cannot become my disciple."[10]

We are fragments of God, little embryonic persons, in whose hearts lie the absolute mystery of the divine abyss. Since we are finite, we feel this central darkness as both mystery and terror. We fear falling into nothingness and grasp at whatever pseudo-certainties we can. *They are all idols.* Certainties always are. The best among us, those who can still see and feel and think with the heart, do the best they can to stand against the tides of arrogance and fear that sweep so many along into violence and despair. They try to tell us that the world is beautiful: beautiful and terrible and desperate and divine, and that it calls to us to *live*, and that this life courses through us at each and every moment, whether we feel it or not, and that it is the ability to breathe these winds of life that is the measure of our being.

———————

Henry Corbin's work is an elegant and extended plea for us to commit ourselves to the perpetual struggle to save the Abrahamic religions from idolatry and literalism, and give them back to soul, to Imagination, and to Life. The spiritual rebirth of which he speaks is an awakening to the inner, imaginal meaning of the Biblical and Qur'anic symbols that have had such a fundamental influence on so much of human history. It is the tragedy of the prophetic tradition that the disruptive and shocking voices of the prophets are heard only as pronouncements of immutable laws rather than as intensely personal warnings and calls for transformation. The prophets and the angels alike serve to rupture our complacencies and unsettle the fixed and fixating lower self. They fragment the stable constructions of the arrogant and willful *ego*, and in so doing, remind us that we are but shards, bits and pieces of the transcendent hidden God, the Black Light at the center of reality.

At the heart of Corbin's message is this dazzling juxtaposition: *Alchemy is the sister of Prophecy.* The prophets call us to transformation. The visitations of the Angel Holy Spirit, the Paraclete of the Gospel of John, de-create us by their presence, so that we may learn to live in the state of constant undoing that defines spiritual poverty and that is necessary for the alchemical opus.

C. G. Jung has awakened us to the psychological meaning of alchemy. Corbin shows us the spiritual meaning. But as both well knew, it is also a physical process. Alchemy is concerned with *matter*, with the stuff of creation. Not as a precursor of chemistry or physics, but as a form of psychosomatic and psychospiritual work. The figure of Christ stands as an exemplar of the Stone that the alchemists sought. Christianity's central metaphor is Incarnation. The central project of Christianity is carnal knowing, embodied knowledge.[11] Incarnation is a *verb*. And it is a project for every one of us.

Corbin's vision tells us that the Gospel of John holds the heart of the tradition, as does Sura XVIII of the Qur'an. In Chapter 14 of John's Gospel, Christ says, "... [H]e who believes in me will also do the works that I do; and greater works than these will he do ...," and later, "... [T]he Holy Spirit, whom the Father will send in my name, he will teach you all things, and bring to your remembrance all that I have said to you." Jung comments:

> It is easy to see what happens when the logical conclusion is drawn from the fourteenth chapter of John: the *opus Christi* is transferred to the individual. He then becomes the bearer of the mystery, and this development was unconsciously prefigured and anticipated in alchemy, which showed clear signs of becoming a religion of the Holy Ghost and of the Sapientia Dei.[12]

And yet for this project of Incarnation to "make sense" in the most literal way, that is, to enliven the senses and bring about a new birth, we have to understand "incarnate" as Corbin does. That is, we need to learn to perceive with the Active Imagination. The material world and the senses that perceive it are transformed by the imagination. Corbin puts it this way:

> The Active Imagination guides, anticipates, molds sensory perception; that is why it transmutes sensory data into symbols. The Burning Bush is only a brushwood fire if it is merely perceived by the sensory organs. In order that Moses may perceive the Burning Bush and hear the Voice calling him "from the right side of the valley"—in short, in order that there may be a theophany—an organ of trans-sensory perception is needed.[13]

What is true for the visions of Moses is true for the Transfiguration and the Incarnation itself. In the *Acts of Peter* we are told that at the event of the Transfiguration each person present saw the Lord only as each was able to perceive Him.[14] Christ must be there in the flesh, the same flesh that can be crucified and killed and examined in the laboratories, but each person sees him with a spiritual vision that is personal and unique.

Corbin is proudly and defiantly a "docetist." That is to say, he subscribes to what became one of the fundamental heresies in the Christian tradition, namely, that Christ was not truly human, but an "appearance." To that charge of heresy he responds:

> Yes. But … it is a docetism that is far from degrading "reality" by making it "appearance"; on the contrary, by transforming it into appearance it makes this "reality" transparent to the transcendent meaning manifested in it.[15]

Always he is concerned lest the "raw data" of sensation and the history of material causality trap religious experience on the level of literal, uniform, universal Truth. This is his objection to the dogma of the Incarnation: Christ appeared in material history, once, and the New Covenant was established, applying to everyone identically. Then the Truth can be apprehended publicly, and the guardians of the Church become the mediators between the individual and the Lord. In the end, the meaning of the person is degraded into the meaninglessness of statistical truth. Corbin rejects this with a passion. Each of us must be the subject of our own life, not the object of some external authority, whether ecclesiastical, political, or scientific.

There is a challenge given us at birth: to accept the responsibility for our own lives. The only adequate response to the gift of life—to the childbirth struggle endured by the mother of each of us—is to make that struggle our own; otherwise we risk being the passive recipients of our own lives. Incarnation is an act—and it requires accepting the gift and the challenge that it entails to enter fully alive into the world, by giving birth to ourselves as creative and embodied creatures immersed in the fecundity of the world. In alchemy this means having it out with the passions on the battleground of the body. The fight to give birth to the higher self requires the interiorization of the figures of the Mother and Father. And as Jung points out, in the torturous exploration in fecundity that is the alchemical opus, "the pregnancy cravings of the mother are stilled with the peacock's flesh and lion's blood, i.e., with her own flesh and blood."[16] That is to say, the alchemist "*must celebrate a Last Supper with himself,* and eat his own flesh and drink his own blood; which means that he must recognize and accept the other in himself."[17] To escape the prison of the lower soul, the passions, obsessions, and needs must be consumed, and so purified. This process *orients* and allows escape from "vagabondage and perdition." Even exiles are not entirely deaf to the call and blind to the figure of the Angel, and it is through the alchemical work of the imagination that one can begin to hear that forgotten Speech and connect to the fullness of the world. Jung's account of the struggle has often been misread as self-centered and isolating. And surely the opus *is* a lonely undertaking. Yet it is only by such a struggle to hear the voice of the True Prophet that the sympathy required for communion with other beings can be developed.

Without the discrimination achieved through the alchemical processes, none of the elements of the world can be experienced in their interiority—they will always be contaminated by the chaos and the exteriority of the unconscious lower soul. They will always be objects, never persons. Neither other people, nor even the very matter of creation can be experienced in their plenitude without this process of coming to consciousness. We are filled with the undiscriminated darknesses of Earth, Air, Water, and Fire, and are thus buried underneath them. Najm Kubra, a 12th-century Sufi from what is now Uzbekistan in Central Asia, wrote as follows:

> The only way to separate yourself from [these darknesses] is to act in such a way that every rightful part in you comes together with that to which it rightfully belongs, that is, by acting in such a way that each part comes together with its counterpart: Earth receives the earthly part, Water the watery part, Air the etheric part, Fire the fiery part. When each has received its share, you will finally be delivered of these burdens.[18]

And, being delivered of these *as* burdens, we burst open to find that we *are* the microcosm, released into its proper home, returned from exile and full of Persons, full of the otherness, the wild and living diversity of the world. We can sing with Walt Whitman, who exults:

> I find I incorporate gneiss, coal, long-threaded moss, fruits,
>   grains, esculent roots,
> And am stucco'd with quadrupeds and birds all over ....[19]

As in Corbin's vision of an earth in which the Word has become flesh not only in the figures of the prophets, but in all the creatures of the Angel of Earth, Whitman sings:

> A song of the rolling earth, and of words according,
> Were you thinking that those were the words, those upright
>   lines? those curves, angles, dots?
> No, those are not the words, the substantial words are in the
>   ground and sea,
> They are in the air, they are in you.
> ...
> Human bodies are words, myriads of words,
> ...
> Air, soil, water, fire—those are words ....[20]

This vision is open to those who are whole in themselves—the interpenetration of the microcosm and the macrocosm can be lived only by those who have transformed themselves. Whitman says:

> I swear the earth shall surely be complete to him or her who
>   shall be complete,
> The earth remains jagged and broken only to him or her who
>   remains jagged and broken.[21]

This is the Alchemy that is the Sister of Prophecy, a Prophecy that is rupture, iconoclasm, and a call to waken from the sleep of the dead and hear the voice of the Verdant One, the Green Man who is the Incarnate One and the Angel of the Earth. The prayer of the 4th-century North African Bishop Serapion can stand as *the* great cry of the human heart: "We beg you Lord, make us truly alive!"[22]

And so one great task in our Quest for the Lost Speech is the transformation of our embodiment by means of the imaginative work of the alchemical *opus*. The Lost Speech is creative and "aesthetic"—it connects us to the Breath of Life and enlivens all the senses. This is the transformation of the Word into Flesh. William Blake, that great spokesman for an embodied and free Christianity, states the challenge most simply:

> Jesus & his Apostles & Disciples were all Artists—
> A Poet a Painter a Musician an Architect:
> the Man or Woman who is not one of these
> is not a Christian.[23]

THE DESERT BEYOND LANGUAGE

To transform ourselves and our vision of the world, we need forms of perception that are enabled by a language not burdened with the accumulated idolatries and unconscious assumptions of the past. One function of the Revealed Word is precisely to fragment *human* language and so, in this way too, to destroy the idols we erect for ourselves. Hossein Nasr writes of the Qur'an:

> Many people ... who read the Qur'an for the first time are struck by what appears as a kind of incoherence from the human point of view. It is neither like a highly mystical text nor a manual of Aristotelian logic, though it contains both mysticism and logic. It is not just poetry, though it contains the most powerful poetry. The text of the Qur'an reveals human language crushed by the power of the Divine Word. It is as if human language were scattered into a thousand fragments like a wave scattered into drops against the rocks at sea. One feels through the shattering effect left upon the language of the Qur'an, the power of the Divine whence it originated. The Qur'an displays human language with all the weakness inherent in it becoming suddenly the recipient of the Divine Word and displaying its frailty before a power which is infinitely greater than man can imagine.[24]

In a masterful analysis of the Prophetic Tradition, one influenced by Corbin's work, Norman O. Brown has suggested parallels between the language of the Qur'an and, astonishingly, *Finnegans Wake*. He says that in its structure, its allusiveness, its ambiguities, its imagery, and its poetry, it is *more* avant-garde, more *postmodern* than Joyce's merely human text.[25] God's Word unmakes all human meanings, all the proud constructions of civilization, and shocks us out of our complacencies and our belief in all the truths we cling to so tightly. There are two idols in particular that prevent us from opening ourselves to the divinity of the world, and they tend to be mirror images of each other. The two great idols that require transmutation into *icons* are God and the *ego*.

I follow Corbin's lead and speak of the *transmutation* of idols into icons, rather than merely of the destructive shattering of idols, and yet alchemical transmutation *is* a shattering experience. In order to "render the idol transparent," a kind of polishing is required. But it is a polishing of the idolator, not the idol. The kinds of polishing are many and diverse, and most of them are in some sense "shattering." Each of the four elements has its own characteristic operation: *Calcinatio* is a fiery immolation; *Solutio* is drowning and dismemberment; *Coagulatio* is fixation in solidity that may lead to imprisonment or crucifixion; *Sublimatio* may grind to a powder that blows away in air. The language of alchemy hints at the difficulty of the soul-work necessary for the journey towards the light that Corbin invites us to begin.

The Trappist monk Thomas Merton was an exemplary figure in what one prominent student of his work has called the "contemplative counter-culture."[26] In one of his last journals, written when he was actively exploring the relation between Zen Buddhism and Christianity, he wrote: "We are going to have to create a new language of prayer. And this new language of prayer has to come out of something which transcends all our traditions, and comes out of the immediacy of love."[27] It is just such an attempt to find a language of prayer that unites the religions of the Book into an overarching *Harmonia Abrahamica* that is a central task of Henry Corbin's work.

Corbin's vision of the life of creative prayer emphasizes nostalgia and ardent desire for the face of the Beloved Divine. But we should be careful not to take Person in a narrow and excessively human sense. An idolatrous version of the personal God of the monotheistic tradition can stand in the way of our entry into the plenitude of life in which we are immersed. For too many people, "God" has become reduced to the image of an infinite *ego*. The word "God" is so compromised, so covered over with our images and projections, our confused hopes and self-centered desires, that we are blinded to the immensities in which we breathe. The new language of prayer that Merton was searching for beyond all the traditions can perhaps be found by letting go even of the idea of God.

Perhaps it is necessary to be exiles, abandoned in the desert, in order to awaken. Here prayer and poverty are complementary. Merton has written:

> ... [T]he contemplative is ... simply he who has risked his mind
> in the desert beyond language and beyond ideas where God is
> encountered in the nakedness of pure trust, that is to say in the
> surrender of our own poverty and incompleteness in order no

longer to clench our minds in a cramp upon themselves, as if
thinking made us exist.[28]

For this surrender, discipline is required: a discipline of regular, guarded
attention, such as one can develop in certain kinds of open-ended
prayer, or in the meditation of Zen and other forms of Buddhism, or
indeed in the intense concentration of the artist and the poet.

Corbin has said that we can learn to "make ourselves capable of
God." For this we need practice, we need "a practice" that will enable
us to experience those influxes of the divine that exist potentially
all around us at each moment. The work of alchemical imagination
and the work of artistic creation can be such practices. But more
seemingly "public" activities can also serve to disrupt us and reveal
our own complacencies and the idols to which we have become blind.
In our time, these disorienting shocks have included anything that
disrupts the prevailing social structure: the passionate revolts of
minorities, of women, of the poor and the powerless everywhere. As
Brown has suggested, there is much of this at work in certain forms
of postmodernism that have as their goal the deconstruction of
human certainties and the dismantling of oppressive social structures
of all kinds.

Yet the postmodern deconstructive project very often leads to
nihilism, and political activism can become mired in cynicism and
despair. Such failures are a kind of half-way point: even further
annihilation of the ego is required of us. If we let go of the idea of
God, so too must we let go of any idea of ourselves. Corbin calls the
ultimate stage in the struggle in the desert the "annihilation of
annihilation."[29] There is a passage *beyond* nihilism in which everything
is abandoned—even our *expectations*. Notice I did not, quite, say, "Let
go of hope." There is a subtle and crucial distinction to be made here.
Letting go of expectations and the controlling and defensive "neediness"
of the lower soul is not tantamount to letting go of *hope*, nor to
abandoning the search for justice and love. For hope is not the same
as expectation. We can learn from the iconoclastic and radically
conservative Catholic social critic Ivan Illich. What expectation expects
is the satisfaction of the "needs" of the *ego*, and the claiming of "rights."
Hope is something entirely different. If "needs" are childish, then hope
is the flowering of maturity. But merely psychological language masks
the spiritual meaning of these states of the soul. Hope expresses another

order of being altogether. Expectation arises in the world of exteriority, of largely impersonal structures. Hope erupts from within the interiority of the world. Illich writes: "Hope centers on a person from whom we await a gift."[30] Hope is always based upon the possibility of rupture, of unpredictable, uncontrollable gift. Hope, the gift, and the person are all, properly speaking, eschatological. They require openness to mystery, and have their source, in the end, in that very desert beyond language that lies beyond the "God" whom we "need," "expect," and have constructed. But as we learn from Corbin, such an eschatology is to be realized in the present, in precisely those ruptures and breaks through which the divine may appear.

In order to live in such hope, it is necessary to abandon our childish attachments to everything: to ourselves, to God, and to the world. There is a distinction between childish expectations and mature hopes. It is disastrous to confuse the two and regard both equally as "desires." Beyond neediness and possessiveness is a hope that opens onto compassion and onto a love that does not split into lover and beloved. Beyond the desert lies awareness of the communion of all beings. But, paradoxically, this relation is founded on the experience of the otherness of other humans, and the non-human otherness of all beings who live outside the bounds of human concern. The great 13th-century Zen master Dôgen puts it this way: "To carry yourself forward and experience myriad things is delusion. That myriad things come forth and experience themselves is awakening."[31]

To be present to the world in this way, it is necessary to free ourselves from the delusions of the "God made in the human image" that so often distort the monotheistic tradition. In addition to the negative theology so crucial to Corbin's vision, we also require a strong dose of what the Eastern Orthodox theologian Olivier Clément calls "negative anthropology." Clément writes:

> *An infinite vulnerability is the condition of this unknowing, where the more the known is known, the more it is revealed as unknown.*
> No, the God of Christians is not the summit—reassuring and plain to see—of a pyramid of beings. He is the depth who reveals depths everywhere, making the most familiar creature a thing unknown.[32]

Of course only a Fool would want to live in such ignorance, vulnerability, and poverty. And there is a long tradition of God's Fools in our heritage. Here are vestiges of a vision of spiritual freedom all but covered over by the religion of the theologians, of the Councils, of what Corbin called the Doctors of the Law. Clément describes these figures for us:

> Humility and silence are so many aspects of interior poverty and renunciation. A person uprooted from a settled life, heads for the desert, to become God's nomad. The real desert is within us.[33]

> Some men of the desert become pillars of prayer, settled or wandering. They reject all domestication, even that of monastic communities, in order to opt for the untrammelled liberty of the wild animals. "Men of the hills" on the heights and in freedom.[34]

> The contemplative, like the illiterate person, does without books. Creatures and things in their delicacy and infinite subtlety continually speak to him of God.[35]

> Interior freedom ... makes possible that attentive gaze, stripped of covetousness, which perceives the outward appearance of each object and its secret, and honours it.[36]

When our tools, our technologies, our theories, our beliefs about who we are and what the world is all come to dominate and control our lives, it is time to head for the hills, to retreat from the systems we have made and that now are making us. Taking to the hills, entering the desert, with compassion, with hope, with humility and the immense discipline of freedom—this is how persons are born, this is how true community is made. For the wilderness is not outside the human city. It grows wherever the strangeness of creation erupts, wherever we come awake to the groundless gift beyond the systems in which we habitually live. This is the "beginner's mind" of Zen Buddhism, where everything and anything is cause for pulling up short and wondering: "What is this?! Who is this?! What is going on?!" Fools and Zen masters, the nomads of God, wander as vagabonds, without destination. But what appears as disorientation when seen from the outside may be the trail left by the apprentice Person trying to listen to the voice of the Angel.

The most important thing is for each of us to find our Voice, the Voice that can articulate the Lost Speech. The quest is a personal one, but the result is communal: compassion and communion. This most personal, most central Voice can be found by those who find a way to heed Christ's call to renounce all that they have, to give up even *need*. In the silence that then descends, one can begin to hear the chorus of creation, to find oneself sung into fragments by a music of terrible majesty and reborn with a love and compassion for creation that passes far beyond any human understanding.

CHAPTER THREE

The Flame of Things

ON KNOWING WHERE YOU ARE

I have spent some years trying to understand fully Henry Corbin's marvelous vision of the unity of the religions of Abraham—Judaism, Christianity, and Islam. That unity is based upon a shared story about the revelation of the Word of God. It depends crucially on a cosmology in which the creative imagination plays a central role. The imagination connects us most powerfully to those divine figures who are the intermediaries between this world and Heaven. It is their symbolic language of images that alone can reveal the inner meaning of the Word of God. If we are deaf to their Speech and thus have no access to this hidden meaning, we are homeless in an impersonal world. Corbin writes: "The drama common to all the 'religions of the Book' ... can be designated as the drama of the 'Lost Speech.'"[1] It is our collective tendency to idolatry that makes us unable to understand anything but the literal, that hardens our hearts and has nearly fatally damaged our souls and the soul of the world. Corbin warns us that the history of the West has been the theater for the Battle for the Soul of the World.[2] He calls us to struggle in that long combat by defending the world of the imagination. He bids us to join together in the search for the language of the angels that is the drama underlying the unity of the Abrahamic tradition. It is a thrilling and beautiful challenge.

And so I came to see this quest for the language of the angels as the most important thing. I still think this is a central task for us. But I now see something that Corbin, I am quite certain, took for granted, which I had pretty well missed. I want to quote a passage that will be very well known to some. But try to imagine encountering it for the first time, because it is really rather astonishing:

> If I speak in the tongues of men and of angels, but have not love, I am a noisy gong or a clanging cymbal. And if I have prophetic powers, and understand all mysteries and all knowledge, and if I have all faith, so as to remove mountains, but have not love, I am nothing. If I give away all I have, and if I deliver my body to be burned, but have not love, I gain nothing. Love is patient and kind; love is not jealous or boastful; it is not arrogant or rude. Love does not insist on its own way; it is not irritable or resentful; it does not rejoice at wrong, but rejoices in the right. Love bears all things, believes all things, hopes all things, endures all things. Love never ends; as for prophecies, they will pass away; as for tongues, they will cease; as for knowledge, it will pass away. For our knowledge is imperfect and our prophecy is imperfect; but when the perfect comes, the imperfect will pass away. When I was a child, I spoke like a child, I thought like a child, I reasoned like a child; when I became a man, I gave up childish ways. For now we see in a mirror dimly, but then face to face. Now I know in part; then I shall understand fully, even as I have been fully understood. So faith, hope, love abide, these three; but the greatest of these is love.[3]

For those who may not know, as I did not for most of my life, this is Chapter 13 of St. Paul's first letter to the Corinthians. If you take it at all seriously, you probably have to change your life. Love comes first, before the languages of men or of angels, before all knowledge, before prophecies, before faith. Before everything.

We have to ask what this love is, without which we are nothing. The King James Bible renders the Latin *caritas* as "charity," but that word now carries other connotations. The original Greek *agapé* is perhaps better translated as "affectionate and deep regard," a kind of holy friendship. The same word was used for the feast of communion that the early Christians celebrated along with the Eucharist, and where they shared their breath in a holy kiss, and their food in a holy feast. This is not what is known as erotic love, and yet it is very physical, festive in fact. It is a communion of souls that transcends the finitude of the earthly person, a perpetual attempt to achieve an encounter, Face to Face, that is the threshold of heaven. Such love never ends.

What can be done to find this love? It is quite clear that it is not commonplace. Many different things are called love, but this radiant, intimate friendship is not commonly among them. In the search for love, so many people seem to set out on a more-or-less frantic search for the perfect lover. On occasion, some get lucky, or are graced, I would rather say. But what most of us have to do, rather than searching for someone who fits the contours of our already formed *persona*, is transform ourselves. Each of us has to become the sort of person who is "capable of God," because it is the light of heaven that reveals the face of the Friend. Other persons have to be perceived as icons, thresholds of the infinite. To the degree that this is achieved, all the world is lit with the light of heaven, because all of Creation has a physiognomy. Corbin asks, "... [W]hat would a world without face or features—without, that is to say, a look—actually be?"[4] Our task is to learn to perceive that look and that light.

The iconic reality of the world is evident only to someone who is properly *oriented*, facing in the proper direction. This often requires a real revolution, the transformation of a form of life. To perceive in the right way requires the proper organ of perception, which is, Corbin tells us, the Imagination. Perceiving and imagining with feeling and precision reveal simultaneously both where we are and who we are.

So where are we? The ecologists tell us that we need to know where we live: the animals, the trees, the flowers, the soil and rock that lie beneath our feet, where our water comes from and where it goes. We do need to know these things, not only as physical conditions, but as physiognomic features of the face of things. The story science tells us about where we are always eventually ends up reducing us all to abstractions, and although people appear in the script, *persons* never do.

Another version of our story begins in a Garden, but it says that sooner or later we all go astray. Shortly after the unfortunate incident with the serpent and the fruit,

> ... the Lord God called to the man,
> and said to him, "Where are you?"[5]

That has been the question ever since. We began by hiding and ended up lost.

Let us accept both stories. We do need to know the plants, the animals, the soils, and the stars. That is one crucial way of locating the human City within a more-than-human context. And yet, even as we do this, we may feel homeless. This is because there is something else going on. Henry Corbin says that human beings are not only located; they *locate*. He tells us:

> Orientation is a primary phenomenon of our presence in the world. A human presence has the property of spatializing a world around it, and this phenomenon implies a certain relationship of man and the world, *his* world, this relationship being determined by the very mode of his presence in the world.[6]

The scientists say we are defined by our world. Corbin tells us that our world *is* who we are. What he calls our "mode of presence," that is to say, our spiritual state, determines how we see the world, and even what we are able to see. Whether the world is opaque and full of idols, or whether it reveals the light at the heart of things, whether the world displays as an icon, an Angel, or the face of God in the face of a friend is determined by our mode of presence. It is possible for us to change, to be open to what Corbin calls the "angelic function of beings," that is, their transforming light. This cannot be done alone, but neither is it likely to occur by the passive reception of grace. At least the process can begin with the discovery of where we are to begin with. This requires the use of all our senses, including ones most of us barely know we have.

Paying attention to where we are is difficult. Many of us are easily distracted, and there is so much going on. Unless we deliberately go out of our way to avoid it, those of us who live in modern consumer societies are immersed most of the time in a world cleverly designed to distract, excite, manipulate, and disorient us. But that's only part of the trouble. It has been clear, at least since Freud, that the conscious ego is a sort of mask over obscure physiognomies. These must be uncovered to get a full view of the world in which we really live. The constant working of the psyche just below the threshold of consciousness is just as crucial to a sense of reality as the ecological, social, and political state of the outer world. If we are unconscious of all the forces that influence our behavior, we risk being no more than the ciphers that statistical science tells us we are.

The inner world has a certain priority. While travel in the outer world is always horizontal, the inner pilgrimage has a Center, and so makes orientation possible. To find our way we have to attend to our dreams and visions and the fleeting feelings that run just below consciousness. There are many ways to do this, but they all involve the imagination. Working with images by learning to read and also to write some kind of imaginative literature, especially, I think, poetry, is one powerful means of revealing and altering our mode of presence; it is one primary technique for exercising the spiritual senses. Few are ever trained in the kind of perception that this requires. And it is a sad fact that most of the people who teach literature either do not know or will not talk about how powerful, how potentially transforming, the imagination can be. The poets themselves say so, and we should listen to them.

A poet's attention can discern the territories of the inner world. But it is difficult to learn the skills involved, and the terrain itself is unstable and ambiguous. The boundaries between perception and creation are not clear. If we have learned anything from Corbin, or indeed from Freud and Jung, we know that we don't make up the contents of our dreams and visions. If you have ever struggled to recall and write down your dreams, if you have ever tried to write the sort of poetry that comes from a source beyond yourself, then you will know that the birth of images in language seems to be both discovery and creation at once. The laws of the imagination are such that revelation and transformation are closely interconnected. What you can see is a measure of what you are. And so, by seeing, we are changed.

———————

The great Mexican poet Octavio Paz says: "I do not see with my eyes. Words are my eyes."[7] The uncanny magic of language makes it possible for us to walk into the world that lies just beyond the threshold of our awareness. But visual metaphors can be misleading. Language is not vision, and the inner landscapes that can be explored through its magic are never entirely visual images: they are suffused with moods and feelings and act on the whole body and all its senses. It is a question of *feeling* in the sense that Jung used the term—feeling as distinct from emotion. Feeling is a rational function of the psyche; it involves discrimination and precision in apprehending the depth and complexity of the world. Emotion is irrational, uncontrolled, undiscriminating, often obsessive, sometimes brutal. *Passion* is such emotion in the extreme. Emotion and feeling are generally confused, but the distinction is critical. Emotions control and dominate us, whereas feeling can make us free. The domination of the soul by emotions annihilates feeling. It is feeling that makes possible the whole-body awareness that enables us to be fully alive.

Jung, during the years of his "breakdown," discovered that the most powerful emotions could be transformed into the realm of feeling by finding images that embodied them, and he called this process "active imagination." Some kind of imaginative discipline seems required to begin the arduous process of the transformation that can free the spirit from domination. Without some form of creative imagination, we go crazy. The creative imagination is the animating spirit that keeps the world alive. Mastering the disciplines required for its exercise is the work of a lifetime.

THE THRESHOLDS OF SILENCE

Freeing ourselves from the domination of the emotions is essential for the development of the soul. Emotions have us at their mercy. And yet they seem to be the most personal, most individual feature of our lives. They seem to originate from our deepest self, and make us feel possessive, even as we are possessed. The passions seem to be what is most intensely *mine* and so are mistaken as forces of individuation. But this is a snare and a delusion. Love and hate, despair and joy, all the passions that sweep us up and master us, all these act to erase our individuality and reveal us to be just like everyone else. Not that this is always a terrible thing. There is a sense of community in it. Everyone in the passion of new love believes that no one has ever felt this way before, and in thinking this, we reveal that we are all the same. Just when we feel most intensely that something is uniquely *ours* are we least our true selves. This sense of self-centeredness is characteristic of the "lower soul." Such passions are engendered by our entanglements with other people, and we almost always accuse *them* of being the cause of our distresses. But it is *our* self-centeredness that is at issue. St. Paul reminds us of this when he says that "love is not jealous or boastful; it is not arrogant or rude. Love does not insist on its own way; it is not irritable or resentful; it does not rejoice at wrong ...." It is really a rather exhausting kind of life, being jealous, boastful, arrogant, rude, insistent, irritable, resentful, and pleased at the misfortunes of others. Most of us know how tiring it can be. And it is always someone else's fault. Depth psychologists call this tendency to find the origin of our distress in someone else *projection*. Much of the work of every religion consists in making us conscious of this.

———————

The first step in the purification of the soul is to put some distance between the developing self and these passions. They cannot be blamed on other people, and although they *occur* in me, they do not originate in my deepest self, and so are not really mine at all. They come from somewhere else, and have a life and intentions of their own. If we can stop identifying with these passions—and this can take years— something else begins to become clear as well. Something even more surprising: we do not belong to ourselves. Our true self does not belong to us at all. There really is nothing that is "mine" for there is no "me," in our habitual possessive sense of self. I belong to another. I am nothing in myself, and so can have nothing. Corbin calls this *mystical poverty*. It is also the deep meaning of *metanoia*, the Greek word that the New Testament uses for the revolution, the radical turn of the soul toward God, which is translated into English as *repentance*, a term that has developed a load of unfortunate connotations over the ages. The sin that we are meant to repent of, and the origin of all idolatry, is what the early Greek Fathers called *philautia*, love of self. According to Maximus Confessor, "Whoever has *philautia* has all the passions."[8] We are idolators of ourselves. In a masterful compendium of and commentary on texts from the patristic era, the Orthodox theologian Olivier Clément says that our blind self-centeredness "snatches the world away from God to annex it, making neighbors into things."[9] All the passions are "forms ... of that 'self-idolatry' that deflects towards nothingness our capacity for transcendence."[10]

This diagnosis of the pathologies of our habitual forms of life is radical and traditional at once. It is radical because it goes to the root of the distress that pervades the lives of so many people in modern secular cultures. The claim is that *idolatry* has caused the tragic events that underlie this anguish: the death of God, the death of nature, and the imprisonment of free persons within the walls erected by the desires of the *ego*. If something like this is true, then freedom and rebirth will come only from actions that can dissolve the structures of *philautia*. Here is where another paradox lies. Force will only bring ruin. The destruction of the lower self can be accomplished only by powerlessness, by letting go. Corbin tells us that the opposite of idolatry is not a "fierce iconoclasm." The struggle against idolatry has nothing violent about it at all. It is not destruction, but transformation. It requires "transmuting the idol into an icon."[11] The transmutation of idols into icons is the real purpose of asceticism, of the struggle with the demons of pride and greed and fear, and their multitudinous offspring.

Every religious tradition provides some form of ascetic practice aimed at undermining the dominance of the lower soul. Although Corbin often refers to the struggles required on the spiritual path, his writings provide little in the way of practical help. Jung is a better guide here, and so too are the early Christian ascetics, those Fathers, and the few Mothers who are known, who went into the desert and encountered their passions in the personified form of demons.

The passions are expressions of the deepest wounds to our souls, and facing them rather than letting them dominate us is difficult, sometimes more than can be born. Jung has said that one way to encounter and transform these powers is to engage them in an imaginative interaction, a dialogue—to give form in images and words to their demands and the agonies they cause. This rich and varied theater of the psyche is a powerful technique in the soul's struggle towards freedom. I know this to be true. But I also believe that it has limitations, a fact that perhaps helps explain the deep suspicion of the imagination expressed by many spiritual traditions, including the early Christian ascetics and their modern followers in the Orthodox and Catholic traditions.[12] I still follow Corbin and Jung in their enthusiasm for the imagination. But the creative imagination and the perceptions that it engenders eventually bring us to the thresholds of silence. Both Jung and Corbin knew this, but it is easy to miss in the wonderment that is generated when one first discovers the full-blown reality of the life of the psyche.

I want to contrast two forms of silence, though I am sure a more generous imagination could discover many more. The first may be encountered in struggles with the demonic, with the passions. It comes from what Corbin would call the sub-conscious and what might be characterized as pre-linguistic. It is the silence of the chaotic, mute, and barbaric. It cannot be articulated, only endured. Here is an account from the life of the first known Christian monastic and desert ascetic, St. Antony of Egypt:

> Antony entered one of the tombs, shut the door behind him
> and remained there alone. And the enemy ... came one night
> with a multitude of demons, cutting him and beating him, so
> that he lay on the ground speechless from the extreme pain
> inflicted by the demons.[13]

Twenty years ago I would have scorned the thought that such pathological "nonsense" could have any relevance for us today. Now I do not. The general response of the Christian ascetics to these assaults was simply to take refuge in Christ. Do not attempt to speak with these demons, do not negotiate, do not imagine—just endure and pray for deliverance. In our time it is a great step forward merely to acknowledge the existence of these forces that grip us and to recognize that they have a life of their own. We need not identify with them. We can be released from their power. What makes this struggle with demons *ascetic* is the steadfast and agonizing refusal to give in to them, the refusal to identify with them, the refusal to let them take over the soul. It can feel like a life-and-death battle, in which one really must die in order to win. Generally, a long series of deaths and resurrections seems necessary. Sometimes Jung's techniques work, and we can speak with the figures crowding round. But sometimes it is necessary merely to endure in the face of inarticulate, roaring silence. Then the response to the demonic attempt to possess, obsess, and devour is a counter-balancing silence that comes from what Corbin calls the supra-conscious: a silence beyond and above language and an acknowledgement that we cannot save ourselves and can only turn toward the Angel. If self-love is the mother of all demons, then it is by letting go of the self, by turning toward the Angel, that the demons will be overcome.

A NORMAL LIFE

According to many of the Fathers in the patristic tradition, the final result of long ascetic practice is *apatheia*.[14] The ancient Greek word does not have connotations of "apathy," listlessness and unconcern. It signifies freedom from obsessions, addictions, and

46 AFTER PROPHECY

compulsions. It is a freedom that makes possible the kind of love that perceives transcendence and that has no end. This freedom opens the soul to the world with compassion, with a love that does not fall apart into loving and being loved. And remember that this "love" is better expressed as deep, intimate, festive *friendship* than as the kind of passionate, erotic, so-called "romantic" love that is one of the central pillars of modern culture and the mainstay of modern advertising. Perhaps people whose lives are driven by passions need more things than those who strive to live in friendship.

Though the struggle with demons can be rather dramatic, the form of life that is the result of ascetic discipline is, as the Benedictine monk Aidan Kavanagh says, nothing special, nothing particularly mystical or extraordinary. Whether one's passions rise to the level of demonology or whether the struggle is less theatrical, the goal is the same: to turn the idol of the *ego* into the icon of the true person, with a face turned toward the Angel. This life is very mundane. Kavanagh says, "The ascetic is simply a stunningly normal person" who expresses "a kind of Zen in the art of maintaining a life of 'right worship'" in the face of an abnormal world in which violence, greed, and arrogance have become the norm.[15] Ascetic renunciation is often caricatured as mortification of the body and denial of all pleasure. That it has taken this form is surely true. But the asceticism at issue here has as its goal the activation of aesthetic capacities that lie dormant in all of us. Such an ascetic wants to be rooted, embodied, alive, real. The goal is not "faith in God" or "belief" in a doctrine, or even to discover the "meaning" of life, but the simple enactment of a form of life, a life of "right worship," which provides the living foundation for all doctrine, all belief, all theology, and without which they are empty shells.

This form of life is *orthodox*, for that is what "right worship" means. It is oriented towards the City of God, and all its actions are concerned with *being* rather than with *meaning*. Those of us who have been privileged to become educated were taught to understand what something or someone is in terms of history, material causality, social stratification, psychodynamics, economic determinism, and so on: all the "horizontal" explanations. These ways of understanding operate in the realm of meaning—something is always explained in terms of something else, which gives it its context, which explains it, which accounts for it, which eradicates its singularity and dissipates it among a host of other objects, other forces, other factors, which are somehow elsewhere less present, more general, and therefore somehow more significant than the thing or the person thus explained away. The rational mind is forever asking what something "means"—what is its larger context, where does its significance, its importance, its meaning *really* lie? And so things slip away from us. And we run after them, trying all the while to figure out what everything means.

The goal of this normal life is to stop running, see beyond all these meanings, and perceive the things of the world not as idols but as icons.

The light that illuminates an icon, that illuminates all of Creation revealed, as Corbin says it may be, as one immense iconostasis,[16] does not come from somewhere else. Icons shine with their own light, the light of Heaven. But beware: the light of Heaven is not like the light we know. It does not come from some vast immaterial Sun, some huge, distant cosmic light bulb. If we think that, we have merely expanded the range of the human City and eclipsed the Kingdom of God yet again. The Light of Heaven is not the light of this world at some far remove—it comes from within things and persons in their immanent individuality. It is always here and now, swelling creation with life.

It is not easy to see this kind of light. It is particularly difficult for those of us raised in the culture of the image, accustomed to pictorial representations of the world, and nurtured on the literate and didactic approach to reality that has dominated the West for centuries. But icons are not pictures, and iconic perception does not apprehend pictorially. As Kavanagh says, "Pictures are about meaning. Icons are about being."[17] An icon is an object of prayer and contemplation, not a representation of physical reality, or a depiction of a story that can be "understood" in any discursive sense. The icon is a threshold between the human and the divine, a gateway leading towards that mode of being which is most present, most personal, most God-like. Cultivating the iconic regard, the kind of seeing that allows us to perceive iconically, is a fundamental moral and aesthetic endeavor in the development of the human person. If we cannot see in this way at all, we cannot see other persons, and we can barely be persons ourselves. Ivan Illich, that great overlooked genius of the Western Church, puts it this way: "The icon ... cultivates my ability to see the misery of a slum, or to be present on a bus, or during a walk through the streets of New York."[18] The slow perfection of this kind of seeing is the only way in which we can come to see face to face. Such love never ends.

Asceticism, and the attentive, contemplative life that is its foundation, are coupled in Christianity with the abdication of power in the sacrifice and death of Christ. Thomas Merton puts this in the starkest possible terms:

> The way to contemplation is an obscurity so obscure that it is no longer even dramatic. There is nothing in it that can be grasped and cherished as heroic or even unusual. And so, for the contemplative, there is supreme value in the ordinary everyday routine of work, poverty, hardship and monotony that characterize the lives of all the poor, uninteresting and forgotten people in the world.[19]

This is, it must be said, as problematic for Merton, who became world-famous, as it is for us. Few will want or be able to act on this vision of the completely obscure and humble life, but it does remind us of all those whom Christ came to befriend and honor and bless. It does serve to orient us toward the center of life. I grew up in a small rural town, midway between Boston and New York. In our adolescence, my friends and I often felt marginal, our lives monotonous and uninteresting. We had the sense that better, more significant, more interesting things were going on just over the horizon in those magnetic Cities of Man. I think this sort of sense tends to permeate our entire existence, so that life here and now becomes somehow peripheral. We often want to get to Heaven for much the same reason that I wanted to get to New York. This feeling is very hard to eradicate, but it stands as an obstacle to a deep understanding of the nature of the City of God, where the periphery is nowhere, and the Center, everywhere.

Honoring and enacting to whatever degree we are capable the life of obscurity, simplicity, and poverty of which Merton speaks can point us toward the heart of things. He writes:

> At the center of our being is a point of nothingness which is untouched by sin and illusion, a point of pure truth, a point or spark which belongs entirely to God, which is never at our disposal. ... This little point of nothingness and of absolute poverty is the pure glory of God in us. ... It is like a pure

diamond, blazing with the invisible light of heaven. It is in
everybody…. I have no program for this seeing. It is only given.
But the gate of heaven is everywhere.[20]

In Merton's description of the contemplative goal, in Henry
Corbin's account of mystical poverty, and in Zen Buddhism, there is
a shared sense that the primal state of the human person is utter
emptiness. For Shunryu Suzuki, the founder of the first American Zen
center in San Francisco, this state is more primordial than any religion,
and is a necessary protection against all forms of idolatry. In an
extraordinary statement that gets at the root of the meaning of *faith*,
he says:

> I discovered that it is … absolutely necessary, to believe in
> nothing. … No matter what god or doctrine you believe in, if
> you become attached to it, your belief will be based more or less
> on a self-centered idea. … So it is absolutely necessary to believe
> in nothing. But I do not mean voidness. There is something,
> but that something is … always prepared for taking some
> particular form. … This is not just theory. This is not just the
> teaching of Buddhism. This is the absolutely necessary
> understanding of our life. Without this understanding our
> religion will not help us. We will be bound by our religion, and
> we will have more trouble because of it.[21]

What Suzuki is suggesting is not that we should refuse to take the
doctrines of religion *seriously*, but that we should not become trapped
by them. It is the function of this essential *faith* to loosen our obsessive
attachment to beliefs, not deny them.

The freedom conferred by the ability to let go of doctrines and
rules, and to conquer the idolatry of the self, not only makes love
possible, but is also deeply tied to our ability to both perceive and
create beauty in the world. The architect Christopher Alexander relates
this wonderful story about Soetsu Yanagi, who

> … tells of his visit when he was young to the workshop of an
> elderly Korean maker of wooden bowls. The old man was a great
> master, and Yanagi describes his awe at being allowed to meet
> the master. As he describes it, he went to visit, and was horrified
> to see that the old man, so much revered, was using green wood
> to turn his bowls. At first he does not dare even to mention it—
> since any question about it would imply a criticism—but finally

he plucks up his courage, and says to the master: "You are using green unseasoned wood—and the sap is still flying out of the bowls as they are turned. Will it not cause the wood to split, and check, and crack?" he asks. The old man, without turning a hair, simply says, "Yes, sometimes." And the young man, again, hardly dares to say what is on his mind, but finally plucks up his courage, and stammers, "But, but what happens then, what happens if one of the bowls is checked or cracked?"

"I patch it," says the old man, calmly, and goes on with what he is doing.

That is all. It does not mean that the old man doesn't care about the bowls he makes. But he is deeply relaxed about it, not panicked. And in this state, where nothing is quite so important, nothing is so terribly, heart-twistingly vital, he knows he can let the greatest beauty show itself ....[22]

Relax! The old man does not even have to say it. He simply embodies it. We are not trying to get anywhere. Everything we need is at hand. The center of the world is not somewhere else. It is not to be found by following the rules for making a bowl, it is not to be found in the doctrines of religion (though they may point to it), it is not to be found in New York, or Boston, or in any human city. The City of God is always here and now.

Such a relaxed and generous form of personhood establishes a foundation for the perception and creation of beauty in the world. Part of the essential message of the Abrahamic religions is that only a person can unite Truth, Beauty, and Goodness.[23] In his own profound analysis of the artistic creation of beauty, Alexander has come to the same conclusion: a beautiful thing is always a mirror of the true Self. He argues that at the deepest level, anything with profound life, and that is therefore a mirror of the Self, and hence beautiful, "will always be isomorphic to nothingness—it will have the same structure as emptiness."[24]

This freedom that comes before all religion and out of which all religion arises is a primordial human capacity. It isn't even "zen." The American poet Gary Snyder, for most of his life a student of Zen Buddhism, puts it this way:

I stay with zen, because sitting, doing zazen, is a primary factor. Sitting is the act of looking in. Meditation is fundamental, you can't subtract anything from that. It's so fundamental that it's

been with us for forty or fifty thousand years in one form or
another. It's not even something that is specifically Buddhist.
It's as fundamental a human activity as taking naps is to wolves,
or soaring in circles is to hawks and eagles.[25]

The emptiness at the heart of things is the birthright of everyone.
But we lose touch with it because it is so simple, so subtle, that it
disappears in the crowded tangle of actions and passions that
characterize our "fallen" life. Beyond the passions, after the demons
have been overcome, there is nothing. And in this nothing there is
freedom. The gate of Heaven is everywhere.

A FLASHING IN DARK SKIES

In many traditions, the contemplative state is described by means
of metaphors of darkness. Henry Corbin has written extensively of the
black light that envelopes the mystic in some forms of Islamic
mysticism.[26] The American Zen master Philip Kapleau writes, "The
Great Round Mirror of Wisdom is as black as pitch." The
Enlightenment of which the Zen practitioners speak "comes out of
this 'darkness,' not out of the 'light' of reason and worldly
knowledge."[27] A fretful grasping after knowledge will only hinder the
search for real connection with the world. Shunryu Suzuki says,

> Instead of gathering knowledge, you should clear your mind. If
> your mind is clear, true knowledge is already yours. ... This is
> called emptiness, or omnipotent self, or knowing everything.
> When you know everything, you are like a dark sky. Sometimes
> a flashing will come through the dark sky. After it passes, you
> forget all about it, and there is nothing left but the dark sky.
> The sky is never surprised when all of a sudden a thunderbolt
> breaks through. And when the lightning does flash, a wonderful
> sight may be seen. When we have emptiness we are always
> prepared for watching the flashing.[28]

So here is the return of the image, the *vera imaginatio* of which the
alchemists speak. It is in the purified heart that true imagination takes
place. Henry Corbin has warned us that the *imaginal* world about
which he has written so much does not include all images and all
imaginings. And the early Christian ascetics treated the phenomena
of the human imagination as suspect at best, demonic at worst. Yet

the *purified* heart is open to the world in its fullness. Heyschius of Sinai tells us: "The heart that is freed from imaginings ends up by producing in itself holy and mysterious thoughts, as on a calm sea you see fish leaping and dolphins gamboling."[29] So we begin like the sky, in which a hawk may soar, or the sea, in which dolphins may play, by eliminating the scattered thoughts that diffuse our concentration. There must first be the empty sky, the immeasurable sea, in order for the images to appear, those images which are the words in the language of the angels.

———————

We all emerge, at every moment, out of nothing. Out of the darkness comes the light. So-called "civilized" people are generally so removed from the immediacies of experience by the buzzing confusion that their lives and minds have become that they are unable to appreciate the stunning realism of ordinary life. One purpose of *ascesis* is to uncover that lost reality. Anthropologist Paul Radin comments:

> ... [P]rimitive man feels that reality is given to him in a threefold fashion. He is born into it; it is proved by external effects; and it is proved by internal effects. He is thus literally living in a blaze of reality. ... Primitive man in no sense merges himself with the object. ... What he says is simply this: not all the reality of an object resides in our external perception of it.[30]

Stanley Diamond argues that an archaic sense of immersion in reality is common to the indigenous peoples in non-technological cultures, to artists, and to mystics. They share a heightened awareness of the uniqueness of the individual thing which "commands a focus on the singularity of the object to such a degree that everything seems at once marvellous, strange, familiar and unexpected. No category can exhaust such an object; it saturates the perceiving subject." The artist shares with the ordinary person a focus on the individual object, "but for him the object has become incandescent. He is perpetually recovering his primitivism."[31] This experience of plenitude lies at the root of all our perceptions.

The enlightenment experience of the Zen practitioner is a return to this sense of reality. To quote from an account of one such experience: "Never before had the road been so roadlike, the shops such perfect shops, nor the winter sky so unutterably a starry sky. Joy bubbled up like a fresh spring."[32] Olivier Clément, in speaking of the fruits of the contemplative experience of the Christian ascetic, quotes Vladimir Maximov: "Miraculously … it was as if I were seeing the forest for the first time. A fir tree was not only a fir tree but also something else much greater. The dew on the grass was not just dew in general. Each drop existed on its own. I could have given a name to every puddle on the road."[33] This is, says Clément, to see everything "in God." For the most part we do not see the world this way; we do not have the eyes for it. Orthodox theologian Paul Evdokimov laments our misunderstanding of the nature of creation: "… [W]e have lost the flame of things and the secret content of simple reality."[34] He writes:

> The image of the Burning Bush or the "flame of things," according to the expression of St. Isaac the Syrian, receives its full luster: St. Maximus says that "the unspeakable and prodigious fire hidden in the essence of things, as in the bush, is the fire of divine love and the dazzling brilliance of his beauty inside every thing."[35]

To recover the flame of things, to see the earth as an angel, and God in the face of the lover, we have to release ourselves from the passions and find the freedom that this confers. Then we *are* the dark sky and the open ocean. Then we are open to the light and to the images that are the language of the angels. We perceive the world as an icon to the degree that we ourselves have become transparent. Then we may see face to face.

In an address delivered five months before his death, Henry Corbin reminded us that in the Old Testament, the angels are recognized by their eyes of fire. In almost the last public words that he spoke, his challenge to us was that we open *our* eyes of fire.[36] It is through their gaze that we perceive the angelic function of beings. If this is mysticism, it is a mysticism of the immediate, and it shows us what a normal life could be. In one of the most vital passages in his great book on Ibn 'Arabi, Corbin wrote that the angelic function of beings is to prevent us from misunderstanding transcendence by separating it from the beauty of the world and of those we love. For it is through these alone that transcendence is manifested.[37] Such Love never ends.

CHAPTER FOUR

The Cross of Light

Ten Thousand Suns

Born to Protestant parents, Henry Corbin was educated in the Catholic tradition, graduating at the age of 19 from the Catholic Institute of Paris, and subsequently studying with both the Neo-Thomist Etienne Gilson and Louis Massignon, two of Catholicism's foremost figures of the 20th century. But he was profoundly ecumenical, at least from his early university days, and was as familiar with Reformation theology and contemporary Protestant thought as with the Catholic tradition. And his interests were not restricted to the Christian West. He devoted most of his life to editing, translating, publishing, and commenting on medieval Islamic mystical and theological manuscripts. He was one of the great Platonists of the modern world, standing in the long line of Christian theologians, beginning with Augustine, who have held that all knowledge is divine illumination. Corbin in his maturity always presented himself as a Protestant Christian.[1] But his account of the nature of Christ, his Christology, is unorthodox, to say the least. Revelation of the divine light at the heart of things, which Corbin calls *theophany*, always comes through the mediation of angelic figures. Corbin's Christology, as he puts it, "moves against a background of angelology."[2] This angelology is integral to his sweeping vision of the sequence of prophetic revelations from Adam to Mohammad, which he adopted in part from Islamic

sources. Corbin's "angel Christology" has its setting within a general
doctrine of prophetology, which is the unifying theme for the entire
Abrahamic tradition.

These ideas are not unique to Islam, although they are developed
at length by some Islamic theologians. They can be found in the early
Christian community. As Corbin often pointed out, the development
of Christology took place within a Jewish-Christian setting. This has
since come to be widely accepted. The many and varied early
conceptions of the divinity of Christ occurred within the context of
Jewish belief in a variety of figures who mediate between the human
and the divine.[3] Corbin regarded the early history of Christianity as
the setting for choices with regard to the status and function of these
mediating "angelic" figures, choices that would be fateful for the history
of the West.

In the first three hundred years after Jesus, Christianity was
anything but a unified phenomenon. It included, if one can imagine
this, an even wider array of beliefs and practices than it does in the
modern world.[4] An honest survey of what is loosely called Christianity
today sometimes makes one wonder what sense there is in using the
term at all, and this was far truer in the ancient world. There was no
New Testament—in fact, no canonical scripture at all, no uniform
creed, no official doctrine, no Councils to establish the tenets of the
faith. There was, instead, a variety of communities, which accepted
an array of very different writings as authoritative, engaged in an
assortment of liturgical practices, and had an enormous range of
interpretations as to just what being a follower of Jesus meant, what
it required, and what it promised. In the relatively few non-canonical
works that managed to survive from these early centuries, there is a
wealth of conflicting ideas concerning the teachings and the meaning
of the life of Jesus, and it took much thought, time, and political
maneuvering to organize anything like a single, coherent Christian
Church from this profusion of communities. In the competition to
establish what would become orthodoxy there were winners and losers.
From the point of view of the winners, this early diversity was a terrible
confusion of heresies. But many modern scholars, as well as the more
adventurous among ordinary believers, find in this assortment of
Christianities rather a treasure house of imaginative riches. However
one feels about it, one thing is certain: the history of the West would

have been quite different if some other New Testament had emerged, if some other Creed and dogma had reigned triumphant. Corbin was among the early scholars to recognize that one might find in this profusion some paths not taken that perhaps should have been.

In particular, Corbin believed that the eventual adoption of the doctrine of the Incarnation by what became the official Church was a dreadful mistake, the consequences of which are only now becoming clear. In brief, his charge is this: a belief in the literal entry of God into public history and so into social and material reality inevitably ends up secularizing the sacred; and, because the facts of God's sojourn among us can in principle be publicly known by everyone, there can be, and indeed must be, a social and inevitably a political organization whose function is to transmit the Truth of God's Word to the faithful, and so to mediate between God and the individual. And although he nowhere to my knowledge says so explicitly, implicit in his entire ecumenical project is the charge that the Incarnation relegates Judaism, Islam, and any other religion to provisional or second-class status at best. For Corbin, such an authoritarian and political religion is in fact no religion at all. But it is worse even than that. The institutionalization of religion makes it almost impossible to remember that we are each made uniquely in the image of God and have our being only through personal connection to our Lord. Corbin warns us that when the unique and individualizing image of the personal God becomes entirely public and common, that is, when it becomes an idol, then individuals themselves will no longer exist—there will no longer be *persons*.

In place of the doctrine of the Incarnation Corbin proposed not merely a different Christology, but a Christology entailing a metaphysics that radically undercuts all the dualisms that have characterized much of Western thought. He found evidence of such a Christology in the early Church as we know it from the apocryphal New Testament.[5] In the non-canonical *Acts of Peter*, the apostle speaks to a group of the faithful about the Transfiguration he had witnessed on Mount Tabor. All he can say of it is: "I saw him in such a form as I was able to take in." As they begin to pray, some blind widows in the group beg Peter to pray for the restoring of their sight, and Peter tells them to perceive in their mind what they do not see with their eyes. The hall becomes filled with an invisible light that shines into the eyes of the blind women, who then stand up amidst the prostrate group, their sight restored. When they are later asked what they saw, some say an old man, others a youth, still others a boy. This phenomenon lies at the heart of Corbin's theology. He writes:

> We are dealing with visions, theophanic visions. There is actual perception of an object, of a concrete person: the figure and the features are sharply defined; this person presents all the "appearances" of a sensuous object, and yet it is not given to the perception of the sense organs. This perception is essentially an *event of the soul*, taking place *in* the soul and *for* the soul. As such its reality is essentially *individuated* for and with each soul; what the soul really sees, it is in each case alone in seeing. ... The community of vision will be established not by reference to an external object ... but by reason of a dimension of being that is common to this or that group or family of souls. This adequation of vision to the dimension and capacity of the soul in which it takes place is the foundation of what we may call the *metamorphosis of theophanic visions*.[6]

Another non-canonical text, the *Acts of John*, describes a theophany that holds the secret of the diversity of these visions, and of the prophetic tradition itself. It is Good Friday, and while in Jerusalem Jesus is crucified on a cross of wood, in a grotto on the Mount of Olives the Angel Christos appears to the apostle in a glory of light and reveals the vision and the mystery of the Cross of Light.[7] Corbin paraphrases for us:

> This cross is called sometimes Word, sometimes Mind, sometimes Jesus and sometimes Christ, sometimes Door, sometimes Way, sometimes Son, Father, Spirit, sometimes Life and sometimes truth. It separates the things on high that *are* from the thing below that *become* ... and at the same time, being one, streams into all things.[8]

Jesus the man must be distinguished from Christ the Angel. It is the pluriform Angel Christos who appears to each in a form appropriate to each. The Angel is the measure of our individuality. Without such an angelic mediator between the divine and the human, without such a personal companion in Heaven, we would all be no more than what science tells us we are: literal, material bodies in public space, reducible to history and biology. In Aristotle's terms, the Angel

Christos is our final cause. Lacking this, we can have no individuality; we cannot be persons.

The revelation of the Word is metamorphic in a dual sense. Its form depends upon our capacity, but likewise we change in response to the vision. And then, in turn, the experience of the Word will itself change. Revelation as theophany has no fixed form—it is Life, not Death, and it is a Way, not a Thing. The revelation of Life is not the static object of a public Creed. Corbin contrasts "dogma" with theophany. This corresponds to the distinction between the literal and the symbolic. There is a form of perception corresponding to each kind of truth. Corbin comments:

> Dogma corresponds to dogmatic perception, simple and unidimensional, to a rational evidence, demonstrated, established and stabilized. ... Theophanic perception remains open to all metamorphoses, and perceives the forms through their very metamorphoses. ... Theophanic perception presupposes that the soul that perceives the theophany ... is entirely a mirror, a *speculum*. ... It was necessarily a complete a degradation for the word "speculative" to end by signifying the contrary of what the visionary realism intended to announce in the etymology of the word: *speculum*, mirror.[9]

The speculative experience required for the vision of the Cross of Light entails a Christology that has long gone by the name Docetism, from the Greek *dokeo*, meaning "to appear," but also, "believe," "think," and "admit." Corbin says that the term should not be taken, as it often is, to signify "phantasm" or "appearance" in the sense of unreality. The point is not that the visions are "subjective" (in the modern sense) and therefore false and unreal. On the contrary, they guarantee the objectivity of the individual in the only way possible, by grounding the person not in the social and public world, but in the transcendent realm. It is not the case that the Docetic conception requires that Christ only appeared to suffer and die on the Cross. On the contrary, the deepest meaning of the Crucifixion can only be personal and transformational. Corbin quotes C. G. Jung: "The historical facts are real enough. ... Yet ... the act of crucifixion is a mystery, a symbol that expresses a parallel psychic event in the beholder. ... [T]he Docetism of the Acts of John appears more as the completion of the historical event than a devaluation of it."[10]

Corbin uses the term docetism in a broad sense, in contrast to the narrower definitions that are the targets of orthodox polemics. The central issue is the question of the nature of Jesus. He could be one person, either merely a normal flesh-and-blood human being specially favored by God, or an entirely Divine person so that, as the orthodox view would have it, his sufferings really are only some kind of sham (as the Monophysites in fact claimed). Or he could have a dual kind of existence, and this becomes especially problematic. He could in some manner be two *persons* (as the Nestorians held), or he could in some way be one person with two *natures*, as the orthodox position would have it. Corbin says that docetism is not really one doctrinal option somewhere in this confusion. It is

> not a set doctrine but a tendency. Thus it can be reconciled with
> formulations that literally contradict one another: it can go hand
> in hand with a complete affirmation of human reality because
> what it perceives is at the same time not this reality; or it can—
> and prefers to—volatilize this reality (thus going from
> Nestorianism to extreme Monophysitism); or, lastly and better
> still, it can conceive of the reality of a body intermediate between
> the sensible and the intelligible.[11]

According to Corbin, any version of Docetic Christology is a species of Angel Christology. The divinity in Christ is perceived uniquely by each of the faithful, and this is theophany. For Corbin all theophany requires the mediating Form of an Angel. But as we have seen, it is not a passive reception of an external reality. Because of the dual form of the metamorphoses of theophanic visions, the revelation of Christ requires a corresponding "exaltation of humanity." The consequence is that

> human nature ceases to be a "nature" as such and becomes a
> wholly transitory state: man is called, by right of his origin and
> if he consents, to an angelomorphosis, ... his acceptance of which
> precisely regulates his aptitude for theophanic visions.[12]

The call to transformation is not restricted to followers of Jesus of Nazareth. An angel Christology gives a radically pluralistic meaning to these words of Christ: "No one comes to the Father except but by me."[13] Corbin's strategy is to show that there is a continuous thread of docetic angelology running from Judaism, through Christianity, and into Islam. He focuses on the Jewish-Christian Ebionites, adherents of one of the "lost Christianities," whose doctrines were of importance, directly or indirectly, for the development of Islamic doctrine. The central idea is that of the True Prophet, that multiform angelic figure who appears uniquely to each, a figure described by one ancient source thus: "Running through the ages since the beginning of the world, he hastens toward the place of his repose."[14] The creation of Adam marks the first appearance of this Anointed One, the Adam-Christos, destined to appear in the succession of prophets Enoch, Noah, Abraham, Isaac, Jacob, Moses, and Jesus—and Mohammad. Crucially, for Corbin, Mohammad does not mark the end, and we are really only at the beginning of Corbin's version of this story. He found in the Shi'ite doctrine of the Imams, culminating in the Hidden Imam, an angelology entirely consistent with mystical Protestant theologies, based not on the Incarnation but on a post-Pentecost religion of the Holy Spirit. The Adam-Christos appears in the Gospel of John as the Comforter, the Paraclete, and this same figure takes the form of the Hidden Imam in Shi'ism.

In an essay presented at the Eranos Conference a year before his death, Corbin described this Angel Holy Spirit as the figure who shatters monolithic monotheism.[15] The shattering occurs because our only access to the One God is by means of our own individual Lord— we are destined to angelomorphosis as partners with our Angel. Each of us has a Lord, as there are uncountable stars in the heavens. Corbin quotes approvingly from the novel *Erewhon Revisited*, by the 19th-century Anglican, Samuel Butler. The narrator tells us that the Erewhonians had been told about astronomy, and that

> all the fixed stars were suns like our own, with planets revolving round them, which were probably tenanted by intelligent living beings. ... From this they evolved the theory that the sun was the ruler of this planetary system, and that he must be personified, as they personified the air-god, the gods of time and space, hope, justice, and the other deities, ... They retain their old belief in the actual existence of these gods but they now make them all subordinate to the sun. The nearest approach that they make to our own conception of God is to say that He is the ruler over all the suns throughout the universe—the suns being to Him much as our planets and their denizens are to our own sun. They deny that He takes more interest in one sun and its system than another. All the suns with their attendant planets

are supposed to be equally His children, and He deputes to each
sun the supervision and protection of its own system. Hence
they say that though we may pray to the air-god & etc, and
even to the sun, we must not pray to God. We may be thankful
to Him for watching over the suns, but we must not go further.[16]

This "pluralist cosmic theism" sketched by Butler is foreshadowed,
according to Corbin, by the late Neo-Platonist Syrianus, who was
Proclus's master. Syrianus wrote:

If one reaches a grasp of the Sun and the Moon, each of the
properties that this definition will have attributed to each of
these beings, will belong to all the suns (and all the moons),
even where there would be ten thousand suns, for in their Idea
they would all be identical one with the others.[17]

This grand cosmology explains why every encounter with the Angel,
as Corbin says,

puts us in the presence of a known and limited God (known
because limited, and *vice versa*): Angel-Holy-Spirit, Angel-Adam,
Sun of our world,—and of a God unknown and unknowable,
God of Gods, of which all the universes and all the galaxies are
the *sensorium*.[18]

And so we are left with this marvelous image of a living cosmos replete
with countless Angelic suns, each a Cross of Light paired with a human,
or even non-human, soul, of whom it is the celestial companion; all
alive and sensate within the unknowable God of Gods. This vision
displays what Corbin calls the paradox of monotheism: the Absolute
God of the monotheistic traditions can reveal Himself in the finite
world only through a multitude of Heavenly forms.

This vision of the potentialities within traditional monotheism
releases us from a narrow, Christocentric view of history and salvation.
It provides a way of understanding how religious vocation and
revelation could be individually absolute and yet wholly incompatible
with fundamentalism and intolerance.

Docetism robs the Incarnation of its literalism. But also, according
to the orthodox, it robs Christ of His body. The question concerns
how one might conceive and experience the presence of Christ. The
Incarnation as it came to be interpreted by the Councils marks the
unique entry of God into history and is the central event in that history

for what became orthodoxy. Corbin devoted many pages throughout his writings to critiquing the doctrine of the historical, material union of God and man in the person of Jesus. And yet never in any of his published writings, as far as I am aware, does he mention that other central tenet of Christian faith and practice, which commemorates and re-enacts the embodiment of Christ, the Eucharist.[19] But he does provide us with an image of an event that corresponds for him to the function of that sacrament.[20] This occurs in his book on Ibn 'Arabi in passages in which he discusses the intimate relationship between God and his creatures. The basic experience that he describes is of an interdependence between Creator and Creature: God knows Himself through His creation, and the creatures know their true Selves only by finding, knowing, and loving their Lord. The knowledge of God that this implies is passionate and embodied. Knowledge of this sort is for Ibn 'Arabi and for the Sufi tradition, a kind of "taste." And it is with metaphors of food and hospitality that this relation may be described. The Breath of God gives life to all of Creation, and the creatures *are* this breath. This energy of love moves from Creator to creature and back again. The Breath of Love is *food* for both the creature and his God. This gives rise to a continuous mystic Supper, represented in the Book of Genesis by the divine visitation to Abraham in the shade of the trees at Mamre.[21] The three strangers whom Abraham welcomed to his table have been interpreted in Islamic tradition as the angels Gabriel, Michael, and Seraphiel. In Eastern Orthodoxy they represent the persons of the Trinity. This scene is the subject of Andrei Rublev's 15th-century masterpiece, "The Old Testament Trinity." Corbin follows Ibn 'Arabi in regarding this event as a symbol of the Feast at the heart of Creation:

> ... [T]o feed God's creatures on Him is to reinvest them with God, is therefore to make their theophanic radiance flower within them; it is, one might say, to make oneself capable of apprehending the "angelic function" of beings, to invest them with, and perhaps awaken them to, the angelic dimension of their being.[22]

This sharing of the Breath of Compassion as food for Creator and Creature is always visible to those who have eyes to see, and is the cosmic sacrament at the heart of Creation. It is the universal Eucharist, and stands to that sacrament as the Cross of Light stands to the cross of wood.

The Word Made Flesh

Some people will feel that this is all quite wonderful. Some will
be scandalized. There is grandeur in this vision of the world and our
place in it, to which few people with spiritual sensibilities will be
entirely insensitive. It provides a powerful way to imagine an
ecumenical and tolerant future course for the prophetic tradition. But
it does leave questions. I want to talk about one constellation of
problems inevitably associated with Docetism that was largely
responsible for its rejection by what became the orthodox Church in
the first centuries after Christ. If the doctrine of the Incarnation is
abandoned, how does this change the meaning of human embodiment,
and of history?

To present the thrust of the orthodox complaint as I understand
it I can do no better than to quote from Olivier Clément's summary
critique of Monophysitism. As we have seen, Corbin suggests that a
pure Monophysitism fully expresses the tendency towards volatilization
that Docetism as a whole displays. Mono-physite means "one nature"—
that is to say, Christ had only one nature, so that his humanity is
absorbed fully into the divine. The fundamental idea, according to
Clément,

> is to celebrate the transfiguration of all things in Christ. That is
> true eschatologically, "in mystery", (and in "the mysteries", the
> Church sacraments). Secretly the world is already the "burning
> bush", everything is in God through Christ's deified flesh, a "glass
> torch". But this sacramental indicative requires an imperative in
> the ascetic, ethical and historical field. What is offered to us in
> Christ, in the "mysteries", we have to realize in our freedom, in
> the "newness" of the Spirit. Whereas Monophysitism, which is
> irresponsible, quietistic, almost magical, in interested only in
> transfiguration, and that immediately. History is done away with
> or disqualified. ... If Christianity had become Monophysite ...,
> the human dimension of history, humanity's tragic and creative
> freedom and the reality proper to the created being would have
> had difficulty in asserting themselves. ... Christianity would
> have forgotten the Semitic sense of the body and of history ....[23]

A grasp of these criticisms is important for understanding the position
Corbin defends. Even in his most Manichean and "gnostic"
pronouncements, Corbin is not guilty of these charges. There are those

whose idea of spirituality is in fact irresponsible, quietistic, and magical. Often what passes for "New Age" religion is other-worldly in this sense, as is often the case with the popularized Western versions of Eastern religions. This is a danger that a docetic Christology must guard against. A religion that degenerates into escapism has succumbed to denial and fantasy, and can have no understanding of the Creative Imagination that makes it possible for us to perceive the light at the heart of creation. Authentic mystic vision is rare, and it is neither escapism nor denial.

To begin with, the docetism that Corbin defends eliminates any schism between matter and spirit. It is a doctrine of "spiritual realism." The material world is continuous with the spiritual and is in itself neither illusory nor evil. The material and the spiritual lie at opposite ends of a continuum. As one moves from the lower to the higher, the dense to the subtle, one's center of balance shifts, and the center of gravity alters. Spiritual reality is the source of the true substance of things. When metaphors of weight and gravity are used to suggest the significance of a person or idea, this is implicitly recognized. Subtle bodies are not vaporous phantasms but are heavy with a fullness of being and meaning. But that does not imply that the material world is a realm of demonic darkness as some Gnostics believed. Our dense and resistant world is less subtle, *less* real than Heaven, to be sure, but it is not for that reason insignificant. It is the fruit of the creative activity of God. The purpose of this world is not to provide a launching pad towards Heaven. It is an expression of the fullness of Being, necessary for the great drama of descent and return, its purpose perhaps, as John Keats claimed, to be a "vale of soul-making." Corbin's fondness for finding support for this cosmology in certain early Christian Gnostic texts should not obscure the fact that he does not adopt the world-denying anti-materialism and loathing for the body that they sometimes express, and against which the early proto-orthodox Christian apologists argued so vehemently.[24]

Now we come to the heart of the matter. What really protects the spiritual realism of this angelic prophetology from the charge of quietism and irresponsibility is the central place it gives to spiritual transformation. Secretly, the world is already a burning bush, but the quest is to *see* it that way, and to *act* as if one saw it that way. As Clément says, this requires active participation in the "ascetic, ethical and historical field." The metamorphosis of theophanic visions depends upon the participation of the whole person. Alchemy is one manifestation of that struggle. It is "the sister of prophecy," according to some in the Islamic tradition. I am speaking of spiritual alchemy, as it has been understood by Jung, Corbin, and the spiritual alchemists in the prophetic tradition. It is a process of bringing to consciousness the spiritual realities that remain hidden from the natural soul. This alters what Corbin calls our "mode of presence." It is a kind of "spiritual hermeneutics." "Hermeneutics" means "interpretation," which sounds pedestrian enough, but the Greek root refers to Hermes, the guide of souls, and in the Christian West the term was applied exclusively to the exegesis of the Word of God. Alchemy is a means of orientation by which we begin to see the inner reality of the Word as it lives, personified, within us. It makes it possible for us to perceive the Angel, and so become ourselves.

One of the fundamental dynamics of alchemical work is what Jung called "withdrawing projections," a clinical term that rather conceals the agonies involved. To put it as simply as possible, withdrawing projections involves disengaging ourselves from the passions, from the complex and varied emotions that drive most of us almost all of the time, in order that we might be free to learn to *feel.* Feeling is something very few of us are able to do. Poets can often do it—and poetry is a species of alchemy. The American poet e. e. cummings puts this with rare clarity. He says,

> A poet is somebody who feels, and who expresses his feelings through words.
> This may sound easy. It isn't.
> A lot of people think or believe or know they feel—but that's thinking or believing or knowing; not feeling. And poetry is feeling—not knowing or believing or thinking.
> Almost anybody can learn to think or believe or know, but not a single human being can be taught to feel. Why? Because whenever you think or believe you know, you're a lot of other people: but the moment you feel, you're nobody-but-yourself. To be nobody-but-yourself—in a world which is doing its best, night and day, to make you everybody else—means to fight the hardest battle which any human being can fight; and never stop fighting.[25]

These words express the struggle for reality that is the essence of the alchemical opus. Corbin often speaks of our existence in exile and our longing to go home. This does not express a desire for escape from life—

rather, the opposite. The longing is *for* life. It is a desire to bring about the intense reality of the present moment, the most intimate and personal encounter with the world.

Now, it is fairly easy to understand what cummings is saying with regard to thinking, believing, and knowing, because they are clearly something very different from feeling. Or so we think. They are, in reality, most of the time dominated by emotions. Think how passionate people are about the things they think, believe, and know. So we immediately get entangled with emotions, even when we think we are not. But if even thinking, believing, and knowing get muddled up with emotion, it is far more difficult to grasp the difference between emotion and feeling. Emotions are the deep forces of nature coursing through us; they are wild and inhuman, like the thunder, like great storms at sea, and the howling of the wind. They do not belong to us. They will, if we let them, destroy us, and those around us. Sometimes the destruction is literal, but often it occurs more subtly, as our spiritual birth is aborted. The goal of alchemy is the transformation and humanization of these impersonal forces of nature. During the long, dark struggle, a faint spark of consciousness takes fire and is slowly differentiated from the matrix of the natural soul. We may, if we are graced, finally imagine that we stand in a clearing in a dark wood—the spark grown to a body of light, freed from the compulsions that rule the unconscious soul.

Some of us, myself included, are fascinated by the bizarre and mysterious aspects of the alchemical literature, but this can be a distraction. A familiarity with the imaginal language of alchemy is an invaluable guide to the processes that go on in the psyche. But it is our mundane, everyday engagements with other people that provide the occasions for the most difficult and potentially productive alchemical procedures. I think of the institution of marriage, which can provide an effective alchemical vessel for the working out of psychic and spiritual struggles. Some of us are habitually blind to the spiritual potential of everyday life, and this explains the longing for escape from the mundane chores of living. Some hope that Heaven will come down to meet them, and so they wait passively for salvation to come from Elsewhere. But spiritual transformation is not entertainment. We have to engage actively in the world as it is around us at every moment. Spiritual realism means that the real world is here right now. In the kitchen, with the idiots at work, with your children, your wife, your husband, your most annoying relatives—everywhere! This is what keeps us connected to history, and what gives it significance. Even though our slow and painful transformation is measured on a vertical scale, it must take place horizontally, in *time*. History is neither demeaned nor done away with, but it has meaning only because of its relation to events in the realm of the soul. Historical struggle is meaningless if it is merely the eternal repetition of attempts to establish a material utopia, with no attention to the transformation of souls. History has meaning insofar as it is the arena in which spiritual transformation takes place.

Alchemy, of course, is supposed to be about matter—about some kind of work on matter, the transformation of lead into gold. Some alchemists really did work on matter in laboratories filled with flasks and furnaces and a host of fantastic instruments—sublimating, coagulating, putrefying, fermenting, and so on. But the matter worked on by the true alchemists is not literal matter, or not only literal matter; it is some mysterious *substance* that includes within itself the world and the soul at the same time. Alchemy is an attempt to bring to *life* the substance of the world. This substance, the raw material of spiritual alchemy, is provided by the emotions, and emotion is a profoundly physical phenomenon. Our bodies are the site where the passions play themselves out. The alchemical work attempts to bring about the birth of a personal, articulate, differentiated, complex feeling body from the chaos of impersonal and passionate matter.

It was Henry Corbin's contention that the doctrine of the Incarnation has done enormous damage by confusing these issues terribly. The orthodox interpretation has misled us into confounding the distinction between the individual living body, which is a body of freedom, and the public, impersonal body, which is a body of compulsion and of spiritual death. The misunderstanding derives from confounding flesh and matter. Christ was a being of *flesh*, not of matter. Matter is public and impersonal. People conceived of as material objects are fit subjects for control by the institutional, political Church. *Persons*, however, can be guided by no one but the Lord. *Flesh* can only be personal, individual, and "for each one unique." The Word became flesh, and it is this flesh, this personified material substance that is the goal of the alchemical work. Only the personal has weight, the weight of *gravitas*. Only the Personal has *substance*.

People who think about the world like to divide it up into categories of things. As far as I can tell, only theologians, poets, and certain kinds of psychologists still accept the category of the *person*. Everybody else these days is pretty much effectively down to Matter, and perhaps Mind. This is part of the story that explains why the dogma of the Real Presence of Christ in the Eucharist began to be an issue in the 11th and 12th centuries. Corbin points to the rise of Aristotelian categories and the collapse of the Neo-Platonic cosmology, which provided an angelic and imaginal world in which these events of the soul could occur. To accept the category of the Person as a fundamental given requires acceptance of the existence of the Imaginal world, and the central place of Imagination in the cosmos. The question of the Real Presence arises only as the bread and wine become "material substances," severed from the realm of spirit, rather than personified fragments of an ensouled world lying in the hands of God.[26] The Real Presence is a wholly imaginal phenomenon. The Word became *flesh*— not matter. The fact that the Word can become flesh is a measure of what we can call, following Ivan Illich, the "worldliness of the world," a measure of the animation that is accomplished only via the imagination. Only ensouled flesh, only personal substance is real.[27] The material world, if by this we mean a world made of abstract "matter," conceived in the absence of the category of the Person and the personification of things that this makes possible, is not a world properly speaking, but a mechanism.

Alchemy, as I understand it, is a form of life whose goal is the creation of Flesh. Corbin has told us that we can learn to see, not with our natural eyes, which he calls eyes of flesh, but with eyes of fire. Eyes of fire are the mark of angels in the Old Testament. He says,

> To open "the eyes of fire" is to go beyond all false and vain opposition between believing and knowing, between thinking and being, between knowledge and love, between the God of the prophets and the God of the philosophers.[28]

The eyes of flesh to which Corbin refers are the literal eyes, eyes that see only idols, that cannot see into the mysterious blackness of the icon, that cannot give and receive active love, but only ever desire to possess and to know with the unveiling clarity of exterior light. By the term "flesh" I intend something different. The Flesh that is the goal of alchemy is the flesh from which the eyes of fire can be born.

In the final analysis, the crucial elements of the critique of Docetism do not apply to Corbin's Angel Christology. It is neither a form of irresponsible quietism, nor does it imply the denigration of the body or of history. It transfers the work of Christ to each of us in a religion of the Holy Spirit, in which spiritual birth and the transformation of material creation into living Flesh in no way requires a historically unique Incarnation. What it does require is the continual presence of the figure of the True Prophet "running through the ages since the beginning of the world."

THE TWO FACES OF GOD

The psychological and spiritual struggle of alchemy is *work*. Periods of intense depression and paralysis, which the old manuscripts call the "blackness," the *nigredo*, alternate with interludes of a searching confusion, which can take many forms. The seeking involved is effort of a peculiar and subtle kind, demanding patience, sensitivity, and delicacy enough to try the most devoted soul. It demands an intensity of attention required only by forms of life in which the creative imagination dominates. It is not possible to speak very clearly about these things, and this accounts for the obscurity of alchemical writings. Any generalizations are apt to be misleading and the process is best described in images. It is a journey in the underworld, and for the trip one must have a certain faith in darkness. The *nigredo* is intolerable, and from it there seems no escape. But there is another darkness. It is what Corbin's spiritual masters call the Black Light, and to learn to feel it in the underworld is a primary task of alchemy. This blackness orients, and it will open, but only in response to our movement. As one foot is placed slowly in front of the other, the path appears on which to tread. The voice echoes into spaces that emerge and take shape by that very speaking. It is impossible to know who or what will be found there. The upper world in which we are accustomed to living is marked by well-worn paths, and inhabited by figures wearing masks, who are more *persona* than person. In this ready-made world it is possible to live almost entirely as a spectator, even in the midst of active and seemingly engaged lives. But a ready-made existence is impersonal, and such abstraction makes it all too easy to believe that life is driven by random and inexplicable external events. Even spirituality can become impersonal, if salvation is regarded as a pure gift over which we have no influence at all but only the hope of being passive recipients of grace. If we attempt to become oriented by the Angel, all this changes. The search for the Holy Spirit, the search for our eternal Face, is wholly unlike the search for any ready-made being, for what is sought does not lie somewhere out there, waiting passively to be found. It does not yet *exist* in the sense in which we habitually use this word. Mountains exist, and I can go find them, but spiritual realities are not like that. We may wish that they were—that would make things much easier. But this is where the danger of irresponsibility really lies— because the fact is that *we* are responsible for the existence of these realities. That is the burden and the glory of the Creative Imagination. The Angel of our Face, our Lord, exists *potentially*, and our work is to bring about the *act*. The process of creation is slow, halting, unpredictable, and full of doubts and uncertainties. Grace is necessary, and the outcome is not guaranteed. But if we take up the challenge of the creative imagination, we cannot be content with our lives as spectators, but have to wake up and grapple with the substance of the world. The work of alchemy is an intercoursing with the entire world. It can be imagined as a kind of dialogue with a partner who is reticent, difficult, often absent, almost always obscure. It is a kind of prayer. And prayer, as the creative act *par excellence*, "is the expression of a mode of being, a means of existing and of *causing to exist* ...."[29]

This form of dialogical life is profoundly physical. Our bodies are the world lived from the inside, and through them we experience all the elements of Creation. At the heart of existence, there is a dark and unfathomable union of our own innermost substance with the elemental forces of nature. Earth, air, fire, and water are powerful symbols of our deepest being. But the matrix in which we are embedded is not material. The human soul and the elements of material creation achieve full reality only when they are articulated and differentiated through the power of the Voice. And just as there can be no language without a voice to speak it, so there can be no voice without someone to hear. There is no private language. We are embedded, all beings are embedded, in a matrix which is the Breath of God, waiting to be spoken. The opus is an effort to make Flesh from elements of nature brought to life through words of dialogue. In this it mirrors the Eucharist, in which the Word is made Flesh, real and present.

We are liturgical beings and our actions resonate in registers we cannot perceive. The processes of alchemy are steps in the process of becoming the unique Person whose face we were born to bear. The slow dawning of consciousness and the transformation of the natural soul begin to reveal the Face of the Angel. But although the work is solitary, the goal, like the liturgy, is communal. Spiritual birth is never a private matter. The early Christians regarded conversion, the turning around of the soul towards the Lord, as the major *social* task of the Christian community.[30] The Greek root of the word liturgy, *leitourgia*, meant originally a "public duty,"[31] and that is how the consequences of transformation can be understood. Even a glimpse of the Angel can light the whole world so that other people can be perceived as the impenetrable and mysterious creatures that they are. If the prison of the lower soul is never opened to the influx of the divine, the faces of others will never be more than mirrors of the *ego*.

Corbin insists that transcendence is manifested only through a being of beauty—the highest form of this encounter is the relationship with a *person* whom we love. The flesh, which is the final goal of alchemy, is not *my* flesh; it can only ever be *ours*. To attain to the status of Person, we need to abandon the idea of the solitary ego. Just as God is not an object, a greatest Being, so a person is not a thing. The angel whose Face we hope to see, and by seeing, also to *be*, is less an object than a relation, more a *process* than a *thing*. In truth, the Angel is the personification of *feeling*—the concentrated manifestation of the attention the soul pays to the world. Corbin tells us that feelings *induce knowledge* of entities proper to them.[32] The Angel is the active subject of such creative knowledge.

As the traditional concepts of subject and object fail us here, so too do the ideas of higher and lower. It is true that the relation between transcendence and immanence can be expressed by images of hierarchy, but this is only part of the truth. Our relation to the divine is also communal. This is reflected in the Christian doctrine of the Trinity. It reveals an image of a world in which love circulates and binds together a community of unique persons in a pattern of sensitive mutual attentiveness—this communal pattern of Creative Imagination maintains the divine energies in act. This circulation holds the world together from within—it is an image of the energies that bind the higher and the lower together, so that transcendence can shine through the beings of this world. This is one of Henry Corbin's constant themes:

human love and divine love are not in conflict—they are expressions of the same relationship of longing and fulfillment. The opening of the soul releases us simultaneously toward the two Faces of reality, the human and the angelic. They interpenetrate so that we may see each in the other and neither ever separate and alone. As the center of our consciousness shifts from the closed and defensive ego towards the Clearing where the conversation begins in earnest, we discover that we do not belong to ourselves—we are constituted and maintained by both the Angel and the human Friend.

Spiritual transformation is one of the great mysteries of Creation. In the furnace at the root of things, something is forged, something fragile and elusive. Out of that dark there emerges a still, small voice of praise, speaking not of power but of life and active love. The human body filled with the warmth of this love, and listening for the dark voice of the Angel, is finally and at last a body truly made flesh. Or so we Imagine.

CHAPTER FIVE

Touching Grace

INTRODUCTION

From the very beginning of my engagement with Corbin's work I have occasionally felt more than a little ambivalence. I have been alternately both captivated by and cautiously suspicious of various aspects of his vision. One of the chief reasons I became enthralled with Corbin was that he offers us a way to overcome the dichotomy between Matter and Spirit, a way to live poised and balanced in simultaneous awareness of both the immanent and the transcendent. Yet in his writings, the transcendent is decidedly dominant. I have struggled a great deal over the years to keep him from dragging me off into Heaven prematurely. But I believe that it would be a mistake to read him as an entirely otherworldly mystic. The spirituality he describes demands an unwavering attention to the immediate presence of the infinite here and now. Nonetheless, Corbin tells us that our vocation is the struggle to become an angel, and that this should cause us to move in this world as a Stranger, a "prince of the other world" on our way back to our native home.[1] This is not world-denying mysticism, and Corbin is an excellent guide to perceiving the beauties and graces of this world. But there are times when I feel that his longing to go Home is rather stronger than mine. I believe that we must be born with our whole being into *this* world before we can ever go Home.

The world desperately needs Corbin's generous ecumenical pluralism, his rich and liberating imagination, his passion for beauty and longing for love. But I am at times wary of his nostalgia for the Elsewhere and his desire for the Body of Light. Reading Corbin now often leaves me with a strong desire to coagulate, to incarnate and seek some ground. His account of the Imagination punches a hole in the literal world and lets in the light of transcendence—but that light shines upon this world. Few of us are genuine mystics, and the mystic vision is easily misunderstood. Authentic mystic vision is neither escapism nor a denial of suffering and evil. It is, rather, the result of the struggle with them. By opening up a way into the Beyond, it offers a means of entry into the deepest reality of the present. The freedom that transcendent vision offers is both a freedom *for* the world and a freedom *from* it.

I have, for a long time, been in the awkward position of being profoundly attracted to two thinkers whose worldviews collide. I have read Corbin against the work of another unique theologian, also deserving of far greater attention than he has received, Ivan Illich. Illich's immersion in the world of flesh and blood provides a counterweight to Corbin's mystical spirituality. To a significant degree, their differences are a question of style and psychology. In alchemical terms, Illich's dominant process is *coagulatio*, and this stands in stark contrast to Corbin's overwhelming *sublimatio*. The two men think and feel in very different registers. But there are also substantive theological differences that run very deep. In certain fundamental respects, Corbin and Illich could not be any more different. Reading Illich has taught me a great deal about what I think are limitations in Corbin's vision. Corbin's pluralistic, imaginative metaphysics seems to me indispensable. But certain aspects of his mystic vision require, I think, a measure of caution. I have no quarrel with mysticism, and rather wish I were a mystic myself. But one need not be to accept Corbin's theology. I want, paradoxical though it may seem, to accept Corbin's critique of the doctrine of the Incarnation as it was developed by the dogmatic Church, but at the same time to accept the full weight of the world. I want to give equal power to the Biblical and the Qur'anic sense of embodiment and to Corbin's nostalgia for the Elsewhere. We find in Illich an extraordinarily sensitive attention to the imaginal richness of the physical, carnal world. In what follows, I will suggest that it is possible to argue for an Angel Christology that does full justice to the incarnate reality of human beings.

———————

Ivan Illich died in the winter of 2002 in Bremen, Germany at the age of 76. *The Guardian* called him "one of the world's great thinkers, a polymath whose output covered vast terrains."[2] The *Catholic News Service* said, "Ivan Illich was one of the most celebrated, denounced, praised and defamed figures of mid-20th century American Catholicism—a gadfly, a charmer, a ruthless critic, and a truly original, if highly unorthodox figure."[3] He was born in Dalmatia in 1926. His mother's family were converted Jews, and she took her children to Vienna in 1932 to escape persecution. In 1942, they moved to Florence, where Ivan played a minor role in the Italian resistance. After the war, he studied philosophy and theology at the Gregorian University, obtained a Ph.D. in history at the University of Salzburg, and was ordained a Catholic priest in Rome. Though seemingly destined for a brilliant theological career and studies at Princeton, he abruptly chose instead to work as a parish priest among Puerto Rican immigrants in New York. He worked among the poor in Latin America for many years. His later life was devoted to scholarship and teaching, although he was critical of academic culture and never held a permanent appointment at any university. He lived a nomadic life as an itinerant teacher, was fluent in most of the languages of Europe, and moved between Mexico, the United States, and Europe. He was a medievalist of the first rank, and had a special love for the Latin writers of the 12th century. He understood history as the Archimedean point that makes it possible for us to grasp the nature of the changes that have given rise to the culture of the modern West, which he saw as wholly unprecedented and unique in human history. His view of human nature was profoundly conservative, and he was a scathing critic of the fundamental assumptions of modern culture. His work provides an unparalleled guide to the changes that have occurred in our understanding not only of ourselves and the world, but of our very perceptions, and much of his later writing concerns the history of perception, as we shall see. His scholarly specialty was the history of liturgy, and the meaning of liturgy is central to his vision. One of his long-time friends commented that he "understood ... that the most ominous expression of secularization in the West was not the death of nature ... nor a misnamed materialism, nor sexual 'freedom,' but the decline of liturgy, the routinization and emptying out of religious ritual in the churches."[4] His writings cover an extraordinary range of topics and are often dense, enigmatic, and, to my mind, haunting. His work is startling and complex—no summary can do justice to the insights that he provides. But it is his profound humanity that makes his thought so unforgettable.

WHO IS MY NEIGHBOR?

Much of Illich's life was devoted to analyzing and revealing the community-destroying, life-denying effects of the institutions of modern culture. In a world dominated by technologies controlled, or more often let loose, by human acts, we find ourselves victims of what Illich calls "the break with the world." All of reality, all of what used to be Creation, is now organized and manipulated by human agency. The world of sacrament is gone. In one of his bleakest pronouncements, Illich, referring to the great Jewish poet Paul Celan, with whom he felt a considerable affinity, writes that the children of today

> are offspring of the epoch after Guernica, Dresden, Bergen-Belsen, and Los Alamos. Genocide and the Human Genome Project; the death of forests and hydroponics; heart transplants and medicide on insurance—these all are ... tasteless, without smell, impalpable and un-worldly. ... Paul Celan knew that only smoke remains from the world-dwindling that we have experienced. It is the virtual drive of my computer that serves me as the symbol for this irretrievable disappearance, and through which the loss of world and flesh can be envisaged. The worldliness of the world is not deposited like ruins in deeper layers of the ground. It is gone, like an erased line of the RAM drive.[5]

By late in his life, Illich had abandoned his early hope that the course of history could be changed. But in spite of this claim that the worldliness of the world is gone, he never gave up hope for us as members of small and committed communities, analogous in some ways to those of the early Church. In the end, it is not society and its institutions that support us. The only access to the world, and so to God, is through encounters with other people, not *en masse*, but as individuals with whom we choose to recapture access to the grace and beauty of creation.

The meaning of "the worldliness of the world" can be understood only by grasping what Illich means by *flesh*. Flesh is embodied love. In Christ, God became flesh, and the Good News He proclaimed was the possibility of a radical and utterly individual human freedom grounded in the grace of God. In the story that is for Illich the centerpiece of the entire New Testament, "a lawyer stood up and put [Jesus] to the test," asking him, "Teacher, what must I do to inherit eternal life?" "What is written in the law?" Jesus responded. The lawyer replied that the essence of the law is to love God with all your heart and soul and strength, and to love your neighbor as yourself. The lawyer then asked a question that would immediately occur to a lawyer: "Who is my neighbor?" Jesus then related the parable of the Samaritan, who, in what would have been seen at the time as "a shocking violation of ethical decency,"[7] is moved by compassion to help the stranger lying in the ditch.[6] Illich wants us to stop short in our tracks too, as he startlingly opens our eyes to the meaning of this by now well-worn parable. This is not a story telling us how we should behave—it is not the establishment of a rule or a moral code or a "Christian ethic." It is not to be understood as a duty, but a *call*. Illich's friend and colleague David Cayley explains:

> ... [W]hat is remarkable about the story is its revolutionary assertion that the neighbor could be anyone, and that who it turns out to be could, as Illich sa⸴ ., "appear arbitrary from everybody else's point of view." No category ... can define in advance who the neighbor might be. ... What Jesus calls the Kingdom of God stands above and beyond any ethical rule and can disrupt the everyday world in completely unpredictable ways. ... What is revealed in the New Testament, according to Illich, is a summons beyond all cultural or religious containment. "Faith in the incarnate word sacrificed on the cross," he says, "is not a religion and cannot be analyzed within the concepts of religious science."[8]

Christianity is the gift of *radical* freedom to see God in any person whom we freely choose. Love and compassion are necessarily enfleshed, particular and immediate, beyond any abstraction, any rules, any institutions. Christians are called to live in grace and precarious freedom. The Biblical term for this compassion is, as Illich prefers to render it, "charity," from the Latin *caritas*, or, in the Greek of the New Testament, *agapé*—it is a loving friendship that is *essentially* an

individual vocation and a personal call. It is the act by which we claim
our *person*-ality, our existence as images of God, and escape the
impersonal anonymity that characterizes a life dominated by systems
or institutions.

The radically individualizing freedom, and so, of course,
responsibility, that is the meaning of Christianity is for Illich tied to
the literally inconceivable event of the Incarnation of God as a human
being. He shares with Karl Barth the notion that Christianity is, in
Barth's words, "the abolition of religion."[9] The transcendent power of
the Word sweeps all human-centered concerns away. It signals
something "radically and explosively new in the world."[10] Only if this
revelation originates entirely outside the circle of human norms and
rules, and indeed of human experience altogether, can it be free of the
idolatry that compromises all human constructs. The uniqueness of
the Incarnation is precisely what gives it its world-shattering
significance.

And yet it is just here in this glorious gift of compassion, freedom,
and the capacity to realize fully the "glory of being you and me" that
Illich perceives a profound and sobering ambiguity. He regards the
history of the West as the story of the perversion and betrayal of the
message of the Gospel. It is, I think, hard to overstate the radical impact
of his claim. I will let him speak for himself:

> Th[e] central reality of the West is marvelously expressed in the
> old Latin phrase: *Corruptio optimi quae est pessima* [the
> corruption of the best, which is the worst]—the historical
> progression in which God's Incarnation is turned topsy-turvy,
> inside out. I want to speak of the mysterious darkness that
> envelops our world, the demonic night paradoxically resulting
> from the world's equally mysterious vocation to glory.
>
> My subject is a mystery of faith, a mystery whose depth of
> evil could not have come to be without a corresponding and
> contrary height in the history of salvation.[11]

The freedom to love, unlimited by any human rules and norms, releases
a dangerous and volatile divine energy into the world. As Cayley puts
it, "[S]hould this freedom ever itself become the subject of a rule, then
the limit-less would invade human life in a truly terrifying way."[12]
Thus the Incarnation is inherently ambiguous, dangerous, and in fact
apocalyptic. Illich says that whereas for the Prophets of Israel the word

of God took flesh in their mouths, with the coming of Christ "there was no longer any need for the word of God to come through the mouth of any prophet. Prophets, in the strict sense," are no longer necessary.[13] But the new prophets, the apostles, do have a message to announce. It is the presence of a new mystery—the *mysterium iniquitatis*—the mystery of evil, which Paul speaks of in his second letter to the Thessalonians.[14] The message is this:

> ... [T]he final evil that would bring the world to an end was already present. This evil was called Anti-Christ, and the church was identified as the milieu in which it would nest. The Church had gone pregnant with an evil which would have found no resting place in the Old Testament.[15]

The Incarnation brings not only the possibility of a new kind of love, but also a new kind of glorious individuality based upon the recognition of the God-like-ness of each of us as enfleshed divine beings. It also brings the possibility of a new kind of betrayal—for each of us finds our true self only in the presence of the love of the other. It is this new possibility of the denial of the humanity of the other that lies at the heart of the mystery of evil. Illich sees in the manifold horrors of our time the perhaps final development of this inhumanity born along with Christ in Bethlehem. The evil he refers to lies not only in the wars and genocides that scar our era, but also in the pervasive institutionalization of every aspect of our lives. Our world is pervaded and dominated by techniques of manipulation and control that undermine the possibility of encountering another human being as the finite face of God. In an interview with David Cayley in 1997, Illich put it this way:

> The first generation of Christianity recognized that a mysterious type of ... perversion, inhumanity, denial had become possible. Their idea of the *mysterium iniquitatis* gives me a key to understand the evil which I now face and for which I can't find a word. I, at least, as a man of faith, should call this evil a mysterious betrayal or perversion of the kind of freedom which the Gospels brought.
>
> What I have stammered here ... I have avoided saying for thirty years. Let me now try to say it in a way that others can hear it: the more you allow yourself to conceive of the evil you see as evil of a new kind, of a mysterious kind, the more intense

becomes the temptation—I can't avoid saying it, I cannot go on
without saying it—of cursing God's Incarnation.[16]

I quote these startling words with some hesitation. I risk
misrepresenting these anguished words of this most passionate
Christian. It is impossible to appreciate the fullness of his faith without
long familiarity with his writings. He is attempting to articulate in
the starkest possible terms his sense of the utter mystery of the glory
and the horror brought about by the inevitable consequences of the
Incarnation. The Incarnation is to be praised and cursed beyond all
human understanding.

With the birth of God in the flesh, prophetic hope gives way to
faith in the "carnal presence of God." As Illich says, it is no longer
God who comes first: "… [F]or Joseph, the baby came first. Faith in
the Incarnation can flower in our time precisely because faith in God
is obscured, and we are led to discover God in one another."[17] To those
who speak of the God who is the cause of the Big Bang, Illich says,
"… I laugh, and I say, come, let's look at a crib …." For it is in human
relationships that God is to be found.

> Like the Samaritan, we are critters that find their perfection only
> by establishing a relationship, and this relationship is arbitrary
> from everyone else's point of view. … But as soon as this
> possibility is established, it can also be broken and denied. A
> possibility of infidelity, turning away, coldness has been created
> which could not have existed before Jesus revealed this
> possibility. So sin in this sense did not exist. Without the glimmer
> of mutuality, the possibility of its denial, its destruction, could
> not be thought. A new kind of "ought" has been established
> which is not related to a norm. It has a *telos*. It aims at somebody,
> some body; but not according to a rule.[18]

The early Christian community was unlike any community that came
before it. It was not based on any natural or social order, but on the
personal communion of the liturgical kiss, which was a sharing of the
breath, the spirit—the *conspiratio*. It is this possibility that is born
together with *sin*: the possibility of the betrayal of the *conspiratio*. This
ambiguity is essential to the meaning of the community of the Church.
It is, Illich says, part of the *kenosis* of

> God in becoming man and founding or generating the mystical
> body which the Church understands itself to be, that this

> mystical body would itself be something ambiguous. It would
> be, on the one hand, a source of continued Christian life …,
> and on the other hand, a source of the perversion of this life
> through institutionalization, which makes charity worldly and
> true faith obligatory.[19]

Sin is the denial of human dignity. "The idea that by not responding
to you, when you call upon my fidelity, I thereby personally offend
God is fundamental to understanding what Christianity is all about."[20]
The idea of the Good has been perverted. Since the Incarnation, the
good for human beings can only be another person. And since persons
are images of God, they escape all entrapment in norms or rules, and
any attempt to institutionalize human relationships must always go
awry. The Good cannot be treated instrumentally. The history of the
Church, and of Western culture as a whole, is the history of attempts
to institutionalize grace and the call that is implicit in the divine face
of the other person.

> During 1,500 years our entire social and political thinking were
> [*sic*] based on the secularization of the Samaritan, which means
> the technicization of the question of what to do when somebody
> in trouble suddenly surprises me on my way to somewhere else.[21]

SENSATION IN ECSTASY

Both Ivan Illich and Henry Corbin were exquisitely sensitive to the
power of the divine to rupture the fabric of our lives. Both felt in a
powerfully immediate way the perilous ambiguity that results from
intimate contact between the two faces of creation, the transcendent
and the immanent, and both feared the power of impersonal forces to
efface the divine. Both believed that the modern world is on the verge
of losing the ability to imagine and to enact the divine reality of the
human person. For both, it is the fateful ambiguity and instability of
the doctrine of the Incarnation that accounts in large measure for what
has gone wrong in Western society. But whereas for Illich the Incarnation
is the central pillar of the Christian revelation, for Corbin the adoption
of this dogma is the gravest mistake in the history of the Church.

To come to grips with Illich's understanding of incarnation, both
divine and human, we need to consider his discussion of the historical
variability of sensation, of our perception of physical reality. And it is
here that I find perhaps the most important point of contact between

Illich's theology and that of Corbin. I cannot help but read Illich's work in light of Corbin's discussion of idols and icons.

Corbin proposed a vision of the three major monotheisms based upon a fundamental harmony. His ecumenical view of the unity of the religions of Abraham is founded on the centrality of the figure of the True Prophet, the Angel Holy Spirit, whose manifold appearances through time express the diversity of creation and have given birth to the great prophetic religions. One of the central motifs in this grand drama is the prohibition of idolatry. Corbin has defined idolatry as a "spiritual infirmity which consists in either loving an object without transcendence, or ... misunderstanding that transcendence by separating it from the loved object, through which alone it is manifested."[22] The schism between transcendence and immanence that is established by idolatry is the source of both literalism and abstraction. To understand idolatry is to see that literalism *is* abstraction. A realistic and *concrete* perception of the world requires the simultaneous perception of both transcendence and immanence. It must be possible to see both faces of things. There is an essential proportion between the visible and the invisible, and the ability to perceive this connection is based upon *sympathy* as a mode of perception. Corbin speaks of sympathy's "poetic or cognitive function."[23] Only sympathy reveals "the angelic function of a being."[24] It is this angelic function that makes possible "a life in sympathy with beings, capable of giving a transcendent dimension to their being, to their beauty, to the form of their faith ...."[25] Spiritual life is not disembodied. We are incarnate creatures, and transcendence is manifested only in material form: "... [T]here are various ways of turning towards the sensible. There is one that simultaneously and as such turns towards the Angel. What follows is the transmutation of the sensible into symbols."[26] Corbin's "spiritual realism" is perfectly carnal. It is not flesh that is the problem—it is literalism and abstraction that destroy the living Word, that turn the body into an object and love into a merely biological or economic function.

A form of life open to transcendence is immersed in the particular, not the general and abstract. The perception of transcendence does not require escape from the immediate and particular, such as is achieved through the formulation of theories, whether philosophical, scientific, historical, or psychological. It requires the exercise of a certain kind of perception that is rare to the point of non-existence in a technological society. Many of us who live in a media-dominated world risk becoming unable to perceive the inherent uniqueness of the individual persons and things that populate our lives. Modern life threatens to become orchestrated by scripts learned from entertainment and the news media. Though every society has a standard repertoire of social roles, modern capitalism relies on especially pc-verful images cut loose from any of the usual stabilizing constraints that locate the individual in society in a meaningful way. Technological society is based upon the exteriorization of reality. It encourages us to live as automatons in a world of idols. Idolators are not individuals— they are instances of a type. To discover the deeper self requires a different kind of vision. Idols are always abstract and disembodied. Icons are always absolutely particular, unrepeatable, and individual. The perception of icons requires a transformation of the opacity of the idols, and of the self, so that they become transparent to the light within them. The practical question concerns how to learn to see this light, to see with what Corbin calls "eyes of fire." How is the world rendered transparent? How are idols to be transmuted into icons? And, more fundamentally: What does an icon look like?[27]

In this regard, Ivan Illich is indispensable for understanding the historically variable nature of the experience of the flesh and the world of the senses. There are indeed "various ways of turning toward the sensible" and comparative phenomenology can help reveal them. Corbin teaches that an opaque and literal experience of matter and flesh is idolatrous. Illich shows first, *that* modern experience is abstract and opaque, and second, what other sorts of experiences have been possible in the past, and in other cultures. Lacking this historical and cultural consciousness, it is simply not possible to know what is being missed, nor to have any sense of the restrictions of life and experience that the modern world imposes.

Illich's strategy is to use the "mirror of the past." He hoped to call into question all the most fundamental modern certainties about humanity and the world by revealing how different this world is from those that came before it. In some of his later works he focused on the historical phenomenology of our experience of the physical "stuff" of the world, and on the historical variability of sensations.[28] These interests are clearly guided by the centrality of the Incarnation in his thought, and they are of prime importance for our attempt to understand embodiment.

The questions concern the nature of perception: How do humans see? How do we see icons, but also, how do we see anything? And as Illich will make clear in a way quite different from Corbin, intimately related to this question of perception is the nature of the transmutation of idols into icons and how it is effected. Corbin speaks of the development of non-sensible senses, of visionary dream and mystical apperception, of the eyes of fire. Illich characteristically wonders about the history of "the gaze," of the historical phenomenology of the activity of the "carnal eye," the eye of flesh. This fleshly eye has not always been quite the literal organ that the modern Western mind generally assumes it to be. There is more continuity between the eyes of flesh and the eyes of fire than even Corbin imagined.

Against the threat to the integrity of the senses posed by the dominance of the mass media and images in cyberspace Illich wants to "invoke the past to verify trust in the flesh of our senses."[29] He will, with the aid of a host of recent scholars, sketch a history of "the gaze." Phenomenological research has helped to show that perception is not reducible to what modern science tells us it is, and we are interested here not in neurophysiology but in the various ways that seeing has been experienced in other epochs. We will attempt to see the modern, technological world from the outside, using categories that have been abandoned. Illich says that he and his colleagues in this research "assume that the gaze can be a human act." They "wish to explore the possibilities of seeing in the perspective of the good. In what ways is this action ethical?" Against the pressures of the modern world, he is interested in a discipline, an *ascesis*, of the gaze, in order to "explore the conditions for a moral gaze today."

The story begins with a striking claim about the Western approach to images. Iconoclasm is a characteristic and fundamental motivation in Western cultures. From its twin beginnings in Greece and in the culture of the Israelites, through Christianity and Islam, and into the contemporary world, there has been a more or less constant sense of hesitancy in front of the image. This is the thesis of Alain Besançon, a thesis that Illich adopts.[30] The unifying thread in this history is a conflict concerning the representation of the Divine. It is an essentially ethical issue. The philosophical side of the debate, that is, the Greek view rather than the prophetic Judaic view, is the story Illich traces here. The Pre-Socratic philosophers were distrustful at best of the Homeric gods, and the archaic statues of the gods experienced as presences were disparaged in favor of a concentration on abstract entities. "The source of reality is no longer Helios, but fire …. Ideas now stand for the gods." At the end of this part of the tale, with Plato, the paradox that the West still lives with became entrenched. We yearn with our whole being for the vision of the divine, but its visualization is forever beyond our grasp.

But what is this gaze that the ancients turned upon images? We will go far wrong if we assume that they saw in the same way that members of 20th-century technological culture do, or that they saw the same things. The assumption that our experiences are normative for persons in other times and other places is arrogant and simply false. I had the good fortune to learn this in the 1970s from a pioneer and master of this sort of historical phenomenology, F. Edward Cranz. In his words, the modern position "is different from, even alien to, all previous thought, and … there is nothing normative, or even normal, about it, or us."[31] I cannot resist telling an anecdote about this man, whose presence has haunted me all these years. Dr. Cranz was extremely reticent about his thesis that the "ancients" experienced the world in a way radically different from ours. His meticulous and imaginatively close study of texts in Greek and Latin prior to the pivotal year 1100 led him to believe that there had occurred, at that point, a rupture between the ancient and the modern way of knowing and that no one had ever noticed this. The ancients, he said, experienced the world "conjunctively," whereas we experience the world "disjunctively." Although he often said that it shouldn't be possible to ever recapture this vanished way of knowing, since we are so much a product of our time, he was living proof that it could be done, if only fleetingly. He said to me once that as he would sit in contemplation over these ancient texts, sometimes he was afraid that he wouldn't be able to get back to the present. This made me shiver thirty-five years ago, and it still does today. What this taught me was that we are not inevitably prisoners of our time. Thus it was with a strange sense of recognition that twenty-five years later I first read Henry Corbin's claim that we are not in history, but rather history is in us. He says that the past and the future "are not attributes of exterior things; they are attributes of the soul itself. It is we who are living or dead, and who are responsible for the life and death of these things."[32] I am not competent to judge whether the scholarly details of Cranz's account are entirely consistent with the one that Illich provides, but the thrust of the arguments is clearly similar.

The version of the story Illich tells concerns the history of vision. He draws on the work of the scholar Gérard Simon, who shows that nearly everyone who has studied ancient optical treatises has assumed the validity of modern physical and physiological concepts when reading their sources.[33] Simon makes it clear that the subject of ancient and medieval optics is not light, but a ray emitted from the eye, an "effluvium of the pupil." Light, insofar as it is discussed, is understood to be a ray emanating from the sun, the Heavenly eye. None of our modern terms applies to the constellation of events that constituted vision for the ancients. Modern conceptions of subject and object do not easily conform. Simon writes:

> It follows from the exegesis of texts from Plato to Galen that sensation could take place in "ecstasy," that it could occur beyond the limits of the skin. The visual ray was conceived as an ephemeral organ that exists as long as it is actualized by its mingling with the colors brought forth by the light of the sun. Although the soul inhabits the body, not all its potencies are circumscribed by it.[34]

The visual encounter was conceived and experienced by the Greeks as a projection of a kind of flesh into the world, a "dissymmetric intercourse" of the psycho-podium, the limb of the soul, with the color and form of the entities as they are brought to life by the warmth of the gaze of the sun.

Central to Illich's later thought concerning the human experience of embodiment is the idea of "proportionality." The ancient experience of the gaze provides an important example of his meaning. We have no words that will express the pre-modern encounter between a person and the world. For example, our vague and general word "experience" is already too psychological, too internal. We have trouble speaking of this interaction in which "the glance is colored by the world, and the world colored by the glance."[35] It is, writes Illich,

> a cosmic event, the fruit of the fit between two dissymmetric complements. Cosmos comes from *kosmein*, the Greek word for lining up two sides or faces: two armies, shores, sky and soil, eye and colors, ear and harmonic sound. The fit then results in a battle, a river, the universe, *visibilia* [visual images] and music.[36]

There is a natural fit or proportion between our senses and the world in which we dwell, and this relation conferred a "poetic, performative quality" on human existence.[37] This particular sensible, or better, mutually sensitive, proportion is a small part of a cosmic network of correspondences that encompasses this world and the Beyond. Illich says,

> In the world from which we come, and in which in certain residual ways we still remain, things are what they are because something inevitably corresponds to them. … Thomas Aquinas … says that you can't think about anything—any thing!— without knowing that it corresponds in some way to a will that is good, that is essentially good, that something fits it and it fits something.[38]

The loss of this sense of proportionality is what makes the modern world utterly unique. Modern Western culture is the only culture, Illich claims, that one can enter "without the assumption that all existence is the result of a mutually constitutive complementarity between here and there."[39] We have lost the experience of "fit" and proportion, and so have lost what used to be called "common sense," the ability to perceive what is appropriate—what is *good*. What we have lost is a world in which the good, and so moral qualities themselves, quite literally *made sense*.

The next major development in the story we are tracing is the result of the novelty of the Christian attitude towards images. Jesus had from very early in the tradition been called the *image* of God. "The Word of God could be grasped, not only by the ear, but could also be seen, ting[e]ing the gaze with color. Christian hope was oriented to the vision of God's face."[40] And so it is natural to desire to worship the divine image in the icon. But then what is the relation between the artifact, the material icon, and the image of divinity somehow present in it? It was John of Damascus who was instrumental in articulating the first theory of the relation between the gaze and the icon, accepted officially by the Church in 787 at the Second Council of Nicea. Illich gives this summary of the doctrine: The believing gaze is tinged by the appearance of the invisible reality represented; the icon thus leads the gaze from the temporal object to the object in eternity. The icon is a *threshold* between the two worlds. Illich draws on the work of François Böspflug, who has devoted his life to the history of what was known as the *libido videndi*, the lust of the eye. Here it is expressed as a desire for the Divine—the gaze is a "kind of homesickness for the beyond"—this is the eye of Henry Corbin, without a doubt.

But here too, as Illich has shown us before, Christianity has ambiguous effects. In a typically short but powerful comment, he writes:

> This desire to look into eternity has become a constant in western thought, but it has also given rise to the pretension of bringing whatever can be known into the scope of visualization. The *libido videndi* can go in either of two directions: through an icon into the unknown beyond, or into the fascinating artistry of the representative image. One can compare the austerity of an early eastern icon to the succulence of a Velásquez nude.[41]

Of course much has continued to come within the scope of visualization since Velásquez.

The medieval experience was firmly rooted in the tradition of the classical gaze and the world of correspondences. Without these preliminaries, it would seem strange indeed that medieval writers thought of optics as a prelude to ethics. "Gazing, looking, facing, glancing are interpreted as fully human activities that can be morally good or bad."[42] One's character is shaped by the training and formation of virtuous habits of seeing. The guarding of the eye is an ascetic discipline that acts to limit the *libido videndi* in its worldly tendency to open everything to the power of vision. Illich writes, "The training, that is, *askesis*, of the gaze became a necessary condition for the eyes of faith if one hoped to reach out toward the threshold of eternity, the icon. The icon oriented … the gaze. However one needed a certain preparation to look into … the eyes of the image."[43]

Medieval writers began to distinguish clearly between two sorts of illumination as the shift from the classical to the modern began to take place slowly and in stages at around the year 1000. They speak of two kinds of light: *lumen* and *lux*. They describe the *lumen oculorum*, the *lumen intellectuale*, and the *lumen fidei*—these are the morally charged, active sensibilities of a human person. *Lux*, on the other hand, is the light that comes to shine indiscriminately on every object. It will in time give rise to the rational clarity of the Enlightenment. It is a public light that we all see, shining equally on us all. We moderns have lost *lumen* and have only *lux*. As Illich says, "The implications for the possibility of ethics are profound. A person capable of exercising a *lumen* is a far different creature than one passively receiving a *lux*."[44]

The same shift in orientation can be found in the realm of cognition and epistemology as we have traced for the activity of the gaze. Aquinas still presumes the traditional categories. The *intellectus agens* or active intellect "behaves like the visual ray of the classical gaze"[45] and moves outward towards its objects to force them to reveal their universal characteristics. It too is understood as expressing the poetic, performative quality that characterizes all human forms of cognition, whether intellectual or sensible, because all occur in a world composed of a vast network of correspondences. But this will soon change to a situation in which the subject is a relatively passive recipient of emanations from external objects.[46]

The history of the iconic image subsequent to the Second Council of Nicea in 787 C.E. is a story of the division of Christendom. In the Eastern Church, the icon remained a central feature of the liturgy. Illich says that here "the carnal commingling of gaze and *typos* [image] in the icon remained normative."[47] But in the West, the devotion to images never developed to the same degree. Their function as a threshold between human and divine was replaced by a role as substitute for the word. Icons as liturgical entities wherein the gaze could reach out to touch the face of God were supplanted by illustrations of the stories of the Bible for the illiterate, who could neither understand the Latin of the liturgy nor read the words of Scripture in any language. The image gains at once a new opacity as it ceases to be a threshold, and a new clarity as it begins to serve merely as a support, a teaching device meant to explain the spoken or written word. This demotion of the image brings it out of the shadows of mystery and helps to clear the way for the wholly secular uses to which images will increasingly be put. Hesitancy in front of the image has vanished for most believers. Many live now in a culture in which images are all-pervasive, but these have nothing in common with the images defended by John of Damascus and by the Second Council of Nicea. The *libido videndi* now expresses itself entirely in the direction prefigured by the nudes of Velásquez, but in a context in which both the nude and its observer have lost their flesh and become virtual machines, while the gaze is an instrument of amoral power in a vast economic system driven by the will to power, by desire and fear.

But Illich brings his story to a close on a note of fragile and tenuous hope. He pays homage to a man whose work suggests that there may be a future for the other thrust of the *libido videndi*, the desire for the image of the divine. The thought of Emmanuel Levinas provides a guide in this attempt to establish a ground for the recovery of an ethics of the gaze.[48] For Illich, Levinas stands alone in resistance to all the dominant modern trends of visualization: "the disembedding of vision from synaesthesis, the disembodyment [*sic*] of the eye ... the dissociation of the gaze from love."[49] For Levinas "it is the mutual gaze of two persons" that is "the source of personal existence." Let Illich speak—

> ... [T]he face is that which my eye touches, what my eye caresses. Perception of the other's face is never merely optical, nor is it silent; it always speaks to me. ...
>
> ... What the face of the other does in its exquisite delicacy and impenetrability is to address me forever in an ethical way. As he [Levinas] puts it: "I cannot but hear the face of the other, in spite of the profound asymmetry between our faces." Again and again Levinas repeats, "You see and hear as you touch."[50]

What occurs in this mutual gaze is a cosmic event, "the fruit of the fit between two dissymetric [*sic*] complements,"[51] and here, if perhaps nowhere else in the modern world, there is a chance to recover the net of correspondences that has been lost. Here, the fruit of our fit is the birth, in the flesh, of two mutually constitutive persons, where, as Illich says, in "the tactile gaze of your face ... I discover myself as a gift from you."[52]

Prolonging the Incarnation

The Word became flesh. In Greek, *Logos sarx egeneto*. Christianity began with this, in the womb of a very young girl. Illich tells us that before it means "word," *logos* means "proportion" or "fit."[53] There is a proportion between God and every person, and because of this, between each of us and every other one of us. But, and here lies the essential message, between us as fleshly beings—not as abstractions. There is no proportion between me and "humanity" in general; only between me and another actual person, whom I can caress with my gaze, now, in the flesh. "... God didn't become man, he became flesh."[54] To be human, we must touch people.

The parable of the Samaritan is so powerful for Illich because it brings an explosive freedom into the unique and carnal encounters of persons. Illich says,

> The Samaritan has the possibility of establishing a proportion, a relatedness to the other man which is entirely free and conditioned only by his hope that the beaten-up Jew will respond to it by accepting this relationship.[55]

> The Samaritan story makes me understand that I am "I" in the deepest and fullest sense in which it is given to me to be "I" precisely because you, by allowing me to love you, give me the possibility to be co-relative to you, to be dysymmetrically [*sic*] proportionate to you. ... The call of charity, *agape*, which the Samaritan hears ... says that ... the goal of your being ... is in an other whom you freely choose."[56]

What is so powerful here, but so subtle and so difficult to grasp, is the simultaneity of unique historical embodiment and freedom. In the dense and weighty fabric of history, Christ revealed the possibility of freedom from social and natural laws and, through this freedom, the utter uniqueness of the person.

The chance friendship between two persons "drowned in carnality" by means of which each becomes the reason for the other's existence,

> ... is not a spiritual relationship. This is not a fantasy. This is not merely a ritual act which generates a myth. This is an act which prolongs the Incarnation. ... Take away the fleshy, bodily, carnal, dense, humoural experience of self, and therefore of the Thou, from the story of the Samaritan and you have a nice liberal fantasy, which is something horrible.[57]

Horrible, because in the institutionalized liberal Welfare State we are no longer confronting persons, but, to put it as starkly as possible, only abstract, generalized "human beings," towards whom we have obligations and responsibilities. Illich wants us to consider the possibility that there may be little difference between the management of people by churches, governments, and charitable organizations and the management of cattle. When we conceive of people in terms of rules and norms, systems and organizations, then freedom and individuality become invisible, we lose the ability to see the divine in the face of the other, and so we lose ourselves. For I am born only as a gift from you. The proportionality between two persons is an active, performative occasion, giving birth to the flesh of each. Illich says, "I'm enfleshed *through* my acts of charity...."[58] That is to say, our enfleshment must be earned. A spiritual quest that takes incarnation seriously regards it not as a *given* but as the goal of a transformative discipline.

It is our *incarnation* that individuates us. Our free acts of love in their embodied particularity and free uniqueness are the means by which we are born to ourselves. We come to ourselves only through another. The New Testament concept of conversion is conversion "to the Other, the Friend, who is, of course, God become man, but who is known through the one who faces me at the moment."[59] We cannot save ourselves by ourselves. Illich says,

> As a Christian I know that the practice of virtue requires help. In an ultimate sense it requires God's help or grace, but any reasonable reader of the Gospel will understand that that help comes to me through the other who faces me. This is how, concretely, I encounter the Lord.[60]

To reveal what it means to be truly incarnate—that we may live so as to prolong the Incarnation—that is the goal of Illich's work. Christian love, *agapé, caritas*, charity, friendship—this is the most real thing for Illich, this precarious, difficult, dissymmetrical proportionality between two persons. The goal of his entire work is, he says, "to lay the intellectual foundation for an ascetical practice which will foster this relationship."[61] The question is what we have "to renounce in order to live in the present world," what we have to renounce in order to love, what we have to renounce in order to practice freedom.[62]

Here is the paradoxical point of contact with Corbin's Christology. Illich says that in love, in *caritas*, we become incarnate individuals, that we prolong the Incarnation by recognizing the transcendent meaning of the face of another. Our acts of charity enflesh us—they make us real. Incarnation individuates. In apparent conflict with this, Corbin's Platonic theology denies any role for the idea of Incarnation, because it is not perishable and impersonal matter that individuates, but the Angel.[63] But the Flesh of incarnation is not "matter." Flesh has its reality in the imaginal world. The *mundus imaginalis* comes to permeate this world through the experience of love. The experience of conversion that turns us toward the Angel makes it possible for us to love and so to transform impersonal matter into flesh. This revolution turns us away from ourselves and enables us to see the Face of another. The *mundus imaginalis* is the world where Persons are possible and it therefore guarantees the transcendent meaning of love.

Each act of incarnation, every act of love, re-affirms the perpetual availability of the Angel. The angelic function of beings is to make possible the individuation and the incarnation of each of us. To be able to perceive the iconic face of all creatures, to see their angelic countenance, requires an opening that simultaneously brings us closer to the Angel, to other people, and to ourselves. Ivan Illich and Henry Corbin have left us with the same challenge: to see with eyes of fire, to exercise the *lumen*, the gaze of love, in an act of perception at once human and angelic that reveals iconic flesh as the threshold between the human and the divine.

CHAPTER SIX

Words of the Heart

MUNDUS IMAGINALIS: HENRY CORBIN AND THE HIERATIC FORM OF THE SOUL

Near the end of his life Henry Corbin wrote a short essay entitled "Towards a Chart of the Imaginal." It serves as a "prelude" to the second edition of *Spiritual Body and Celestial Earth*, which appeared in French in 1979, the year after his death. In it, Corbin tells us very clearly of the quest and the drama that underlie all of his work. He carefully situates the realm of the Imagination, its power, danger, and necessity. It is worth quoting him at some length. He writes:

> It has been a long time ... since western philosophy ... drawn along in the wake of the positive sciences, has admitted only two sources of Knowledge .... There is sense perception which gives the data we call empirical. And there are the concepts of understanding ..., the world of the laws governing these empirical data. ... [B]etween the sense perceptions and the intuitions or the categories of the intellect there has remained a void. That which ought to have taken its place between the two, and which in other times and places did occupy this intermediate space, that is to say the Active Imagination, has been left to the poets. The very thing that a rational and reasonable scientific philosophy cannot envisage is that this Active Imagination in man ... should have its own noetic or cognitive function, that

is to say it gives us access to a region and a reality of Being which
without that function remains closed and forbidden to us. ...
    Neither the active nor the agent Imagination is thus in any
sense an organ for the secretion of the imaginary, the unreal, the
mythic, or the fictive. For this reason we absolutely had to find
a term to differentiate radically the intermediate world of the
Imagination ... from the merely imaginary. The Latin language
came to our assistance, and the expression *mundus imaginalis* is
the literal equivalent of the Arabic *'âlam al-mithâl* .... While we
encounter in other philosophies or systems a distrust of the
Image, a degradation of all that properly belongs to the
Imagination, the *mundus imaginalis* is its exaltation, because it
is the link in whose absence the schema of the worlds is put out
of joint.
    ...
    ... The Imaginal world creates symbols on the one hand
from the Sensible Forms, on the other from the Intellectual Forms.
It is this median situation which imposes on the imaginative
faculty a discipline which would be unthinkable where it had
been degraded into "fantasy," secreting only the imaginary, the
unreal, and capable of every kind of extravagance. Here ... is
the same total difference already recognised and clearly remarked
by Paracelsus between the *imaginatio vera* ... and "*Phantasy.*"
    ... The seriousness of the role of the Imagination is stressed
by our [Iranian] philosophers when they state that it can be "the
Tree of Blessedness" or on the contrary "the Accursed Tree" of
which the Quran speaks .... The imaginary can be innocuous;
the *imaginal* never can ....[1]

In the absence of the Active Imagination, the phenomena of religious
consciousness disappear, since the Active Imagination provides the very
place of their occurrence.[2] All the phenomena of spiritual life require
the exercise of this Imagination. The *mundus imaginalis* is the
enveloping reality of the entire Abrahamic tradition and is the very
air that all the prophets breathe. Corbin says,

> Upon it depends ... both the validity of visionary accounts that
> perceive and relate "events in Heaven" and the validity of dreams,
> symbolic rituals, the reality of places formed by intense
> meditation, the reality of inspired imaginative visions,
> cosmogonies, and theogonies, and thus, in the first place, the
> truth of the *spiritual sense* perceived in the imaginative data of
> prophetic revelations.[3]

The Imagination provides the means of perceiving the reality of this *imaginal* world, in part by acting as a system of sensory organs that can transform physical perceptions into symbols.

> The Burning Bush is only a brushwood fire if it is merely perceived by the sensory organs. In order that Moses may perceive the Burning Bush and hear the Voice calling him "from the right side of the valley"— in short, in order that there may be a theophany—an organ of trans-sensory perception is needed.[4]

But we should not let Corbin's organic metaphor mislead us. The transformation of sensation into symbol is not an alteration of elements "given" to the mind from an outer world, as in an empirical model of perception. The cognitive role of Imagination undercuts the dichotomy between subject and object. Placing Imagination at the center of human life lays the groundwork for a model of cognition that presumes not that knowledge consists in the accurate representation of an external world, but rather that we are active in constituting reality. Imagination, language, and even sensation are constitutive activities of human beings. Imagination is creative. And in a passage that is perhaps the climax of his book on Ibn 'Arabi, Corbin tells us that it is prayer that is the supreme form of the Creative Imagination. Prayer is a dialogue with the figure of the Lord, who can appear only in a form appropriate to the spiritual state of the soul. Prayer is a means of causing this figure to *be*, and this figure is a real-ization of the mode of being of the soul in contemplation. Corbin says:

> ... [P]rayer is not a request for something: it is the expression of a mode of being, a means of existing and of *causing to exist*, that is, a means of causing the God who reveals himself to appear, of "seeing" Him, not to be sure, in His essence, but in the *form* which precisely He reveals by revealing Himself by and to that form.[5]

This existential link between the human person and the Person of the Lord is expressed in the well-known Sufi saying, "He who knows himself knows his Lord." And as we shall see, Corbin regarded this bond as providing the primary orientation for human life and the foundation for the personal moral imperatives of the religions of the prophetic tradition.

Corbin's account of the power and significance of the Imagination and the *mundus imaginalis* is a passionate defense of the religious and spiritual capacities of human beings. He believed in the world-historical importance of a nearly lost metaphysics that places Imagination at the center of human life, and he devoted his life to bringing it to the attention of the modern world. But he was anxious that his message not be misunderstood. The Western world is perfectly familiar with the products of the imagination, but these tend to be products of a secularized and disoriented imagination, not the *imaginatio vera.* According to Corbin,

> it is impossible to avoid wondering whether the *mundus imaginalis*, in the proper meaning of the term, would of necessity be lost and leave room only for the imaginary if something like a secularization of the *imaginal* into the *imaginary* were not required for the fantastic, the horrible, the monstrous, the macabre, the miserable and the absurd to triumph. On the other hand, the art and imagination of Islamic culture in its traditional form are characterized by the hieratic and the serious, by gravity, stylization and meaning.[6]

Now Corbin was a passionate defender of the most heterodox elements of the Abrahamic traditions. He was a generous and eclectic champion of the imagination, with sympathies covering an enormous range of sentiment, and a partisan of the individual in the face of every form of institutional dogma. His long-time friend Denis de Rougemont remembered his youthful cry, "Heretics of the world unite!"[7] But recalling this same incident some years later, Corbin demurred and commented that what he had probably said was, rather, "Esotericists unite."[8] And in the remarks quoted above emphasizing the gravity and stylization of the traditional Islamic imagination, he revealed again a rather conservative interpretation of the imagination. This raises an issue of enormous importance: What are the criteria that enable us to tell the difference between the imaginary and the imaginal, between *imaginatio vera* and *Phantasy*? Must we appeal only to categories such as gravity, seriousness, and stylization? Or are we hearing in these words the voice of an old man, somewhat irritated at the extravagances of his youth and fearing misinterpretation of his life's work? I tend to think that there may be some truth in the latter possibility. And I believe it is in the spirit of Corbin's life and work to doubt the existence of absolute criteria for distinguishing true imagination from fantasy. But even if there are no public and objective laws governing the Imagination, it is nonetheless important to attempt to fill in the chart of the Imaginal that Corbin has provided, and, in so doing, perhaps begin to orient ourselves at least provisionally in the landscape he has opened up for us.[9]

He warns that access to the imaginal world is not easy—"One does not penetrate into the Angelic World by housebreaking," he says. But what are the alternatives? The question arises for those of us who are not given the gift of mystic vision as to precisely how one "learns the imagination." The initiation can be demanding and prolonged. Corbin lays great stress on the trials of alchemy and speaks of the descent into the underworld, which is the unconscious. He says that we

> must pass through the Darkness; this is a terrifying and painful experience, for it ruins and destroys all the patencies and norms on which the natural man lived and depended—a true "descent into hell," the hell of the unconscious.[10]

But his work provides little practical guidance for our struggles to find the Angel, and he seems to move with ease in realms that often seem remote from the mundane concerns of our fragile and painful daily lives. We need guides in addition to Corbin to help us learn to make the Active Imagination a living reality. If we do not have a veritable Master from one of the great religious traditions to whom we can turn, then we can learn from certain kinds of psychologists, and from the poets, to whom, Corbin has said, the Active Imagination has for so long been relegated. And it may happen that we will be graced with a vision of that unique personal Guide, the only real Master, who is the Angel Holy Spirit, around whom our lives individually revolve.

IMAGINING THE IMAGINAL

Corbin's vision is entirely ecumenical. He considered himself a Protestant Christian and an advocate of a gnostic and esoteric practice, which he believed to be a universal phenomenon. Of this universality he wrote:

> Gnosis was not born in Islam in the Middle Ages, any more than it is a simply Christian heresy of the first centuries of our

era; rather, it is something that existed long before Christianity. There was a gnosis in Christianity; there has been one, and perhaps there still is, in Islam—and perhaps it may yet provide for an unforeseeable spiritual encounter between Orient and Occident. For gnosis itself, in all its manifold forms and variants, also deserves to be called a *Weltreligion.*[11]

By "gnosis" Corbin means "salvific knowledge." It is knowledge that saves by accomplishing the rebirth of the soul in the light of knowledge of the hidden realities of the spiritual worlds beyond.[12] It is in this sense that gnosis is universal—it is not tied to any particular religion but exists as a potentiality within each.[13] Corbin's use of the term "esoteric" is similarly inclusive. Corbin is not an advocate of a particular set of Hidden Doctrines, revealed only to a society of the spiritual elite. His point is rather the opposite—esoteric truth is truth that is inherently individual and individuating. By definition, esoteric truths can come to consciousness and appear only to individuals, and these truths are salvational truths, which accomplish the spiritual birth of the person. Such knowledge can never form the foundation for any social or political group. This brings out the hidden humor in Corbin's youthful call—the very idea of a "union of esotericists" is a bit of an oxymoron. But perhaps we should rather say that a gathering of such individuals would be a true Church, the body of the Lord, a truly spiritual communion of souls, and a "social" entity in appearance only.

Much of Corbin's work is devoted to showing the connections between the spiritual worlds of Islamic and Western mysticism. My interest lies in exploring how we might continue a tradition in which the Imagination plays such a central role in a world which is materialist, skeptical, pluralistic, fragmented, and spiritually exhausted by the manifold incomprehensible horrors of the last hundred years. The foremost questions are: How are we to imagine and encounter the *mundus imaginalis*? and, What are the signs of the *vera imaginatio*? How we answer these questions determines the character of a life lived in pursuit of the Angel. Of the handful of people in the non-Islamic world who have taken Corbin's vision entirely seriously, I want briefly to consider three: C. G. Jung, James Hillman, and Harold Bloom. By contrasting their work with Corbin's, I hope to make more precise our grasp of how Corbin answered these questions himself. Then indeed it will be up to us to continue his work by the exercise of our own creative imagination.

The Shadow of Ahriman

Carl Gustav Jung was a friend and colleague of Corbin's at the annual Eranos Conferences in Ascona, Switzerland. Corbin began lecturing there in 1949, and his familiarity with Jung's psychology is evident in much of his writing. Both Jung and Corbin use the term "active imagination," though it has different connotations for each. For Corbin it is the action of the Angel Holy Spirit in us and it provides our access to the spiritual realities of the *mundus imaginalis*. For Jung it is first of all a psychotherapeutic technique, a means of gaining access to the forces of the unconscious. Jung was generally content to play the role of empirical scientist and forgo speculation about the metaphysical nature of the images that arose as a result of the technique. Corbin, of course, had no hesitancy about the realities of the spiritual worlds in which he moved. Jung was anxious that his psychology be regarded as a science—he was a physician and, as such, a member of the scientific community of the modern West. But though he wanted the approval of his scientific peers, he refused to play by the rules of a materialist culture, and the religious and scientific aspects of his work do not always sit easily side by side. He attempted to show a skeptical world that the spiritual concerns of the past have meaning and relevance for us. In this, and on the central role of Imagination, he and Corbin are in agreement.

But Corbin has left us in no doubt about at least one aspect of Jung's psychology with which he was in complete disagreement.[14] The tradition Corbin upholds gives no positive meaning to the dark side of the soul. He was highly critical of Jung's model of the psyche, according to which we have to somehow integrate our shadow and acknowledge the evil in ourselves in order to achieve wholeness. What is required instead, for Corbin, is *orientation* towards the Angel, who is a figure of Light. Corbin writes:

> Is not the sense of all myths of *reintegration* henceforth affected by this orientation? For the totality of man's being ... is not merely the sum total of orient and occident, of left and right, of conscious and unconscious. The man of light's ascent causes the shades of the *well* where he was held captive to fall back into themselves. Hermes does not carry his *shadow* with him .... And it is difficult, we must confess, to read with equanimity certain interpretations of the *coincidentia oppositorum* where

complementaries and contradictories are apparently
indiscriminately lumped together under the head of *opposita*.
To deplore that Christianity is centered on a figure of goodness
and light and entirely overlooks the dark side of the soul would
be no less valid an evaluation if applied to Zoroastrianism. But
how could reintegration consist in a complicity between, a
"totalization" of Christ and Satan, Ohrmazd and Ahriman? Even
to suggest such a possibility is to overlook the fact that even under
the reign of a figure of light the satanic forces remain in operation
.... And it is exactly for this reason that one has to affirm that
the relationship of Christ to Satan, Ohrmazd to Ahriman, is not
complementary but contradictory. Complementary elements can
be integrated, but not contradictory ones.[15]

Corbin's theological approach presumes an origin for evil outside of
the realm of the human psyche, whereas for Jung *we* are the source of
both good and evil. On Corbin's account, the darker aspects of the
human psyche have to be transcended, not integrated. The reality of
evil must be acknowledged, and the way to counter evil is not simply
to bring it to consciousness, although this surely is a step along the
way. The evils of Ahrimanian darkness are not so readily overcome.
The struggle is not to integrate, but to vanquish. The goal is not a
spurious wholeness compounded of the multitudinous aspects of
psychic life. The realm of the imagination leads not towards a spherical
Homo totus, but rather towards the ever-receding figure of the Angel
who summons us to perpetual transcendences. The process of spiritual
awakening is not one of integration, but of unveiling. The cosmos that
we yearn to know is not spherical and balanced, but open-ended in
an active and lively infinity.

Pathology, Polytheism, and the Three-Ring Circus

Corbin lived to see his work appropriated by others, particularly
through the influence of another friend and colleague at Eranos, James
Hillman. It was the very success of his newly coined term *imaginal*
that caused Corbin to warn against its misuse. He was concerned that
the *mundus imaginalis*, which he had spent so long seeking, would
become lost again through a misunderstanding of the metaphysics that
situates and guarantees its reality. In that late Prelude to *Spiritual Body
and Celestial Earth* he wrote:

> ... [W]e wish to give a caution. We have come to see for ourself
> [*sic*], with pleasure though not unmixed with some anxiety, that
> the word "imaginal" as used specifically in our researches has
> been spreading and even gaining ground. ... If this term is used
> to apply to anything other than the *mundus imaginalis* and the
> imaginal Forms as they are located in the schema of the worlds
> which necessitate them and legitimize them, there is a great
> danger that the term will be degraded and its meaning be lost.
> ... If one transfers its usage outside this precisely defined schema
> one sets out on a false trail and strays far from the intention
> which our Iranian philosophers have induced us to restore in
> our use of this word.[16]

It is clear that Corbin was referring at least in part to Hillman's use of
the term. This is not the place to attempt a summary of the wide-
ranging archetypal psychology of Hillman and those who take their
inspiration from his work.[17] A brief sketch of a few important themes
will have to suffice. Hillman credits Corbin as one of the major
precursors of archetypal psychology and his love and admiration for
the man and his work are evident.[18] But central aspects of his work
are at odds with Corbin's psychocosmology and can perhaps help us
discern the outlines of Corbin's theology of the Imagination more
clearly. Hillman and Corbin differ substantially in their interpretations
of the meaning of polytheism, of the basic model of the psyche, and
of the role of pathology in human psychic life.

Hillman trained as a Jungian analyst, and his work is heavily
indebted to Jung—and of course to Freud. His approach to the psyche
is mythological and polytheistic. He writes:

> The most accurate model of human existence will be able to
> account for its innate diversity, both among individuals and
> within each individual. Yet, this same model must also provide
> fundamental structures and values for this diversity. For both
> Freud and Jung, multiplicity is basic to human nature, and their
> models of man rely upon a polycentric fantasy.[19]

The only theological stance that can accommodate this multiplicity
is polytheism.[20] While Corbin praises the polytheistic project of
H ilman's colleague David Miller,[21] as well as Hillman's first major
book, *Re-Visioning Psychology*, which he calls "the psychology of the
resurgence of the Gods,"[22] there is no doubt that what Corbin means
by "the Gods" is not what Hillman intends. Corbin's "polytheism"

refs to the plurality of individual theophanies of the Angel Holy
Spirit—that figure of the True Prophet, who cannot appear other than
uniquely to each one. He finds a basis for this in Ibn 'Arabi: "Each
being," says Ibn 'Arabi, "has as his God only his particular Lord, he
cannot possibly have the Whole." Corbin comments:

> Here we have a kind of *kathenotheism* verified in the context
> of a mystic experience; the Divine Being is not fragmented,
> but wholly present in *each* instance, individualized in *each*
> theophany ....[23]

The term "kathenotheism" comes from the Greek for "one by one."
In Hindu polytheism, this expresses the idea that each god is, for a
time, considered as single and supreme. But Corbin means that each
individual person has one Lord, not that each person is inhabited by
multitudes. The image he provides is of a universe of "ten thousand
suns," one for each of the ten thousand beings, and reigning over them
all, the Unknown and Unknowable God of Gods.[24] It is quite true,
however, that even one's own unique Lord may appear in a multitude
of theophanies, but these correspond to the variations in the capacity
to *see* that characterize the stages of the spiritual quest. A polycentric
model of the soul and the theology that supports it is far from Corbin's
intent. The Islamic sages whose theologies provide the basis for his
own project never lose sight of the fundamental unity of the Divine,
however much they may revel in the fecundity of the theophanies of
Creation.

The dynamics of the psyche as Hillman sees it are fluid, playful,
and complex, its laws those of a loosely structured society, having
nothing hierarchic or stratified about them. He presents us with a
picture of the psyche as a three-ring circus. He says,

> Everything finds its way back into the tent of the mind, if only
> into the freaky sideshows of pathology. The polytheistic
> gridworks of myths keep all the rings going at once, providing
> the safety nets and stay wires that keep the whole show from
> falling apart. Once we let go the obsessive idea of a single center
> and the idea of order as unity, things can't really fall apart. They
> simply go on performing their variety acts, each according to its
> kind ... round and round, the mind endlessly entertaining, and
> being entertained by, ideas.[25]

This seemingly has nothing in common with the hierarchical architecture of the soul in Corbin's cosmology. There, the primary metaphor is orientation towards the figure of the Angel, who is both the source and the goal for each of us. And yet there is an overlap between the two conceptions, for Corbin's vision is not that of a static hierarchy, and his model of the person has little in common with the Freudian *ego* model, which would make ego defense and the establishment of boundaries the central goals of human psychic life. The unifying center, which is the Face of the Lord, is an ever-receding transcendence and the unity of His theophanies is dynamic. The orientation that the Angel provides is open-ended and powerfully destabilizing. The encounter with the Angel is always a defeat for the *ego*, for the natural soul. Corbin's monotheism is based upon perpetual transcendence and perpetual hermeneutics, and he finds these to lie at the heart of the monotheistic traditions. Hillman, too, acknowledges this pluralism hidden in the monotheistic traditions, in an article written twenty-five years after his original essay proposing a polytheistic model for psychology. He says that in the Sufis and in the Kabbalah there can be found "a polysemous multilayered diversity of images, metaphors and personifications," which can prevent us from succumbing to the "tyranny of unification."[26] He shares Corbin's horror of dogma, literalism, and fundamentalism of every sort. But in Hillman's work we find little patience for the elder Corbin's description of the imaginal world as hieratic and serious, and characterized by gravity, stylization, and meaning.

One of Hillman's chief concerns is to provide a theoretical framework for the practice of psychotherapy. Following Jung and Corbin, he regards the Imagination as the central human faculty. But Hillman's practical need to encompass pathology within his model of the human soul leads him far from Corbin's world. Jung had said that in our time "the gods have become diseases." Hillman writes:

> The link between Gods and diseases is double: on the one hand, giving the dignity of archetypal significance and divine reflection to every symptom whatsoever, and on the other hand, suggesting that myth and its figures may be examined for pathology.[27]

The method *par excellence* for investigating and coping with pathology is imagination. The therapeutic method of active imagination pioneered by Jung is continued by Hillman in a context that makes explicit reference to the *imaginal* world. Hillman comments as follows on the difference between his use of the term and Corbin's:

> Clearly, the pathologizings of the image do *not* belong to the *mundus imaginalis* as he [Corbin] has given us this word. But in the soul-making of actual psychotherapy, pathologizings are often the via regia into the imaginal. ... The refinement of our imaginal sensibility must begin where sensibility itself begins. From the gross to the subtle is an operation, not an ontology. The ontological priority of Corbin's world is nonetheless arrived at via the operational priority of Jung's method—because we must begin where we have fallen, flat on our backs in personal pain. The difference between Jung and Corbin can be resolved by practicing Jung's technique with Corbin's vision; that is, active imagination is not for the sake of the doer and *our* actions in the sensible world of literal realities, but for the sake of the images and to where they can take us, *their* realization.[28]

Corbin equates the Active or Creative Imagination with the Agent Intellect of medieval Christian theology. It is, he says, following his mystical Islamic sources, the result of the action of the Angel Holy Spirit in us. Hillman and Jung both place active imagination at the center of their therapeutic repertoire. The question is whether they are all talking about the same thing. What is the relation between Hillman's practical psychology and Corbin's mystical theology? The answer, I think, is that Hillman has it right in the passage just cited. We do have to start out where we are, in pathology and pain. This is, after all, the procedure of alchemy, and Corbin tells us that the Hell of the unconscious must be passed through. Alchemical texts are replete with bizarre and pathological images, and the blackness of the *nigredo* is utterly essential to the Work. So why Corbin's revulsion at the pathological? The answer surely is that pathology, or in another language, our state as fallen creatures, is only a starting point for Corbin, not a permanent abode. In his book on Ibn 'Arabi he says that our modern arts and even our dreams have become decadent.[29] I take this to mean that our highest aspirations and hopes have become demeaned and degraded. He fears we have lost our orientation. He knows full well the extent of our pathology, and he feels that we are losing the sense that there is any way out. Many in the modern world seem to revel in darkness for its own sake, and this is antithetical to any spiritual quest. Both Jung and Hillman, but particularly Hillman, as practicing therapists, are all too aware of the seeming ineradicability of human pathology. Hillman in the end abandons the kind of spiritual quest that lies at the heart of Corbin's work in favor of a much less oriented and goal-directed approach to human life, one far more accepting of the inevitability of human failings than Corbin's theology could ever be. I suspect that in his cautionary words concerning the potential degradation of the meaning of the imaginal we are hearing Corbin's fears that polycentrism and pathology might come to overshadow the Angel and the battle against the forces of darkness, which threaten to bury the soul of the world.

The Literary Imagination

One defender of Corbin's position, who stands outside both his circle of colleagues in France and the world of depth psychology, is the American literary critic and Yale University professor Harold Bloom. He has presented an interpretation and defense of Corbin's work as part of a book-length study of Gnosticism. It is worth noting that his reading of Corbin is in certain respects quite misleading, and his version of "gnosis" should not simply be identified with Corbin's.[30] In a preface to a new English edition of Corbin's work on Ibn 'Arabi, Bloom argues that we can understand the *mundus imaginalis* as the world inhabited by the great characters in imaginative literature. We have already mentioned Corbin's claim that the Active Imagination has been left to the poets, and his desire to reclaim it for the spiritual life. Bloom, who has, almost exclusively, taught Shakespeare for many years, says that

> ... for our culture, at this time, it may be more pragmatic for seekers to discern the reality of the Active Imagination in Shakespeare, rather than in Ibn 'Arabi or Suhrawardi, though under Corbin's guidance Ibn 'Arabi and the other Sufi sages will help us define the imaginal realm in Shakespeare. ... I don't wish to turn Shakespeare into a Sufi, or Henry Corbin into Shakespeare, but instead link the two in a "process of increasing illumination."[31]

Bloom likens the creation of fully realized figures in the literary imagination with the dialogical creation of the form of the Lord as it can occur in prayer. Both are profound acts of creative imagination.

> The "Form of God"... is as much a dramatic image as a spiritual
> one, and manifests itself when something in us identifies with
> Hamlet or Falstaff. ... Sufic prayer, as Corbin describes it, is what
> can be experienced at very rare moments when we read
> Shakespeare. ... [T]he Sufic "Forms of God" have ... the same
> imaginal status as Shakespeare's greatest characters. The imaginal
> realm is a concept generous enough to embrace both the spiritual
> and the aesthetic. Who anyway can define the borderline
> between gnosis and poetic knowledge? The two modes are not
> identical, and yet they interpenetrate one another. Are we to
> call the gnosis of Novalis, Blake, and Shelley a knowledge that
> is not poetic? In domesticating the Sufis in our imagination,
> Corbin renders Ibn 'Arabi and Suhrawardi as a Blake and a
> Shelley whose precursor is not Milton but the Koran.[32]

For Bloom, the fully realized Shakespearean characters are more
"persuasively alive" than real people, at least, one assumes, the people
whom Bloom knows. A great actor makes the encounter with the
strongest of them "reverberate for a lifetime." These figures of the
imagination are "deeper than life, [with] a wit unmatched by anyone
merely real whom we will ever know."[33] They transcend the human,
as does the Angel. (Bloom's recent pronouncements on Shakespeare
have been controversial, to say the least. A highly entertaining, and to
my mind enthralling, account of Shakespeare and his modern critics
has been provided by Ron Rosenbaum[34]).

What would Corbin have made of this? His works are full of
literary allusions and his fondness for visionary literature from Boehme
to Goethe to Swedenborg makes it easy to imagine him as an
enthusiastic reader of William Blake. But what of his "cautionary note"
and the warning that we must not transfer the use of the term *mundus
imaginalis* outside of its precisely defined schema? Of this passage
Bloom writes:

> As an admirer of Corbin, I am a touch uneasy with this, partly
> because he seems in this moment of fine caution to forget how
> eclectic in their spirituality his Sufis are, and he himself was.[35]

Surely, as Bloom suggests, Corbin would not deny to the poets the
cognitive powers of the creative imagination. The poetic and the
spiritual are linked by a process of increasing illumination, just as the
darkness of pathology and the alchemical opus can lead upwards

towards the light, even if we are not always able to follow. But the issue Bloom raises is central. Corbin's ecumenical treatment of the three major monotheisms is based on the shared phenomenon of the revealed Holy Book and on *hermeneutics*, as the search for the true, esoteric, and personal meaning of the divine Word. Revealed or inspired poetic language is the subject matter of this spiritual Interpretation and so the nature and source of the interpreted text becomes a matter of some importance.

For the believer, the evident difference between *Paradise Lost* and the Qu'ran is that one of them was dictated by God. Both Hebrew and Arabic are holy languages because they were spoken by God. The New Testament stands apart in that there has never been any particular prohibition against translating even the words of Jesus into a multitude of languages. Christian culture is multilingual in a way not possible for Judaism or Islam. But in all these traditions, poets and theologians have had to ponder the relation between human language and the word of God. It is easy for some of us to regard the Torah, the New Testament, and the Qur'an as literary works that can be set on the same shelf as *Hamlet* or *Paradise Lost* or even *Finnegans Wake*, but this is clearly not the case for most traditional believers. How eclectic in our spirituality can we be? That really is the heart of the question. And if your theology centers, as Corbin's does, on the meaning of hermeneutics, then the choice of the text you are interpreting becomes a crucial issue. Corbin accepted the reality of the phenomenon of a Holy Book, and he surely would have had no qualms about the quasi-authoritative status that the works of Rumi have had among some Sufis, nor with the authority of the works of the Jewish commentators on the Torah or the writings of the Fathers of the Christian Church. But he would have rejected the postmodern tendency to regard all texts equally as literary productions, disconnected from any conceivable hierarchic ordering. Corbin would, I think, have agreed that here too there is, as Bloom contends, a process of increasing illumination, which orders a complex hierarchy of poetic imagination in much the same way that alchemical imagery begins in the bizarre and pathological, but is given its orientation by something beyond. To exclude the poetic and literary imagination from the realm of the imaginal would violate the spirit of Corbin's entire life work.

Corbin's critiques of Jung and Hillman have the same motivation, namely, his fear that the essential spiritual dimension of the *mundus imaginalis* will be perverted by the powerfully secularizing and disorienting tendencies in the modern world. The same would apply to the literary imagination in these times, when social and political influences on artists are often given more weight than the aesthetic and spiritual significance of the works they created. The Imagination is our connection to the Holy Spirit, without which we are lost and doomed to wander homeless in a world with no vertical dimension. The tension that Corbin evidently felt later in his life between an allegiance to the free play of the creative imagination and the knowledge that completely unfettered freedom leads to disorientation and confusion is a tension we all have to live with. I do not think that Corbin, or anyone else, will be able to remove our individual responsibility to decide individual cases. The experience of freedom is always disorienting. It is not easy to distinguish between the transcendences to which we are led by the Angel and the chaos that results in nihilism. That is the burden and the task of spiritual hermeneutics—spiritual decisions cannot be made by appealing to rules. But I do think that Corbin's work as a whole provides the framework for a way to balance the conflicting demands of freedom and constraint. Two of the most constant themes in his work are *orientation* towards the Angel, and *perpetual hermeneutics*, which is the unending task of interpreting ourselves and the world so that we do not fall prey to dogmatic certainties and the delusion of absolute knowledge. As long as we are oriented towards the figure of the Angel, whose presence guarantees the possibility of love, we may dare to be generously eclectic without fear of becoming scattered. In the Islamic tradition, this Angelic figure is Khidr, the Verdant One. Corbin says, "He ... who is the disciple of Khidr possesses sufficient inner strength to seek freely the teaching of all the masters."[36]

Perpetual Hermeneutics and the Angel of the Face

The image of the Angel Holy Spirit as the personification of the Active Imagination is one of Corbin's great gifts to us. It is up to us to respond. A spiritual tradition will die unless it is imagined anew by every generation. A theology of the Spirit offers the possibility of personal transformation, but the *act* depends upon us. The question for us is: "What form does the quest for the Angel take in our time?" How can this tradition be interpreted so that it enables the transformation it promises? To be true to Corbin's vision, we have to focus on this word "interpretation"—which is the meaning of the theological and philosophical term *hermeneutics*. The publication in 1927 of Martin Heidegger's *Being and Time* marks a watershed moment for philosophy and theology, and Corbin's encounter with Heidegger's work had a profound impact on his thinking. His reading of Heidegger places the idea of hermeneutics at the center of things. It signifies interpretation as the act of understanding, but not understanding in an abstract intellectual sense. This kind of understanding results in a personal transformation. It is Imagination as the power of the Angel in us that provides the possibility of hermeneutics and so, of human transformation. To respond to the challenge of the Angel, we need to be clear about how the Angel manifests, about the power of the Imagination, and about the meaning of hermeneutics.

Corbin was perhaps misrepresenting his own eclecticism, but his warnings about the seriousness of the imaginal world should not fall on deaf ears. He was right to worry about the misappropriation and misinterpretation of the doctrines that he had worked, for so long, to bring to light. The Creative Imagination is essential for the continued survival of humanity. Henry Corbin was indeed a mystic, and the *mundus imaginalis* is pre-eminently accessible to the mystic vision, but he was adamant that if we lose contact in our everyday life with the reality of the Imagination, we are lost and disoriented, prey to confusion and the forces of evil. The imaginal world is not fantasy and it is not entertainment. It is the source and origin of all that makes us human. The orientation that the Angel provides makes it possible for us to hear the primordial *ethical* call that lies at the root of what it means to be a person. In what follows, I suggest some possible avenues for thinking about the role of the Angel and the Imagination in the modern world.

Human, Non-Human, Inhuman

I want to begin by situating Corbin's theology in the context of a debate between views of human nature that are inherently *impersonal* and those that, like his, are profoundly *personal*. One way to frame the debate is to ask this question: Is the realm of human life and culture autonomous, requiring unique categories of understanding, or are we merely epiphenomena of non-human powers beyond our control, explicable in terms of principles and categories that describe the non-human world? This question defines the dispute between Humanism and Naturalism. Humanism we can provisionally define as a belief in the irreducible dignity of the individual, and the conviction that freedom and responsibility are fundamental categories without which human life is inconceivable. The naturalism that modern science presupposes aims at explaining us in largely biological terms. Naturalism would explain the human in terms of the impersonal mechanics of genes and the contingencies of history. The moral categories that lie at the heart of what it means to be a person remain peripheral and originate in the amoral dynamics of the physical world.

Many will associate naturalism with scientific materialism. But there are other ways to explain the human in terms of the non-human, and I want to ponder another very influential version of 20ᵗʰ-century naturalism. In Davos, Switzerland in 1929, the Swiss, French, and German governments jointly sponsored a gathering of French- and German-speaking intellectuals for the purpose of fostering reconciliation after the horrors of the First World War.[37] The major attraction was a series of lectures by and a debate between two of the leading figures in European philosophy, Ernst Cassirer and Martin Heidegger. Their dispute can be read as one skirmish in the battle between Humanism and Naturalism.[38]

Cassirer was the foremost Neo-Kantian of his time, and his prodigious scholarly output included the three-volume *Philosophy of Symbolic Forms*. He argued for the universal objectivity of human cultural forms of understanding. Human culture is the context for a range of modes of cognition, including language itself, the arts, and religion, as well as science. On his view, these symbolic structures provide ways of knowing that are able to achieve real measures of objective and transhistorically valid truth. All of our modes of knowing depend upon this symbol-forming capacity, the ability to produce meaning, which is the human characteristic *par excellence*.

The young Heidegger's philosophical project was radically different. His epochal masterwork, *Being and Time*, had been published two years previously and his rise to fame was precipitate. On his account, human beings stand irrevocably within history as finite and fated creatures. Our lives are bracketed by our finitude, and unlike any other beings, we are uncannily aware of the inevitability of our own death. We are rooted in the present and are unable to transcend the bare fact that we seem to ourselves to have been cast unwittingly into a world that pre-exists us and in which we are only temporarily present. The Enlightenment dream of a universal and timeless rationality is doomed to disappointment. This is because we are finite and because we are not, in the first instance, rational beings. Prior to the exercise of any rational faculty, we are engaged in interpreting ourselves and the world. That is to say, we are essentially and "primordially" hermeneutic. The world as experienced is always already interpreted. Heidegger's really radical proposal is that the best model for understanding human beings and all of our experience is the act of interpreting a text. Our supposed objective rationality is grounded in a web of pre-rational and non-rational understandings and there is no way to stand outside of this matrix and obtain a truly universal, God's-eye view of Reality. And more than this, as his thought developed after *Being and Time*, Heidegger was concerned to decenter the human subject in the scheme of things. On his account, the human ego as a free and independent subject is largely an illusion. The real actor in the drama is Being—we are at best mouthpieces for the impersonal forces of history as they play out the destiny of Being. The human subject loses any central role in the play of history, and the meaning that inheres in things is discovered by us only by virtue of our participation in Language, which, he will later say, speaks *us* rather than the other way around. Thus, Heidegger will propound, barely two years after the Second World War, that apart from the truth of Being, "man himself does not matter."[39] The most important thing for us is to undo Kant's Copernican Revolution (which conceived of all knowledge as dependent on human categories) and escape our entrapment in the merely human.

Among those present at the Davos debates was the young Emmanuel Levinas. He was to become one of the most significant philosophical voices of the century. Much of his highly original work is conceived in implicit and sometimes explicit dialog with Heidegger. For Levinas, as for Cassirer, Heidegger's reduction of the human to the non-human is yet another version of naturalism, albeit one that is not narrowly rationalistic or reductive in the sense in which science reduces the human to the vagaries of the physical world. But Levinas also rejected Cassirer's prioritizing of culture. For Levinas, the primordial

ground of human existence is provided by neither the pattern of
cultural understanding into which we are born, nor the realization
that we are "thrown" into existence in such a way that we provide the
"clearing" in which Being appears. What comes first, what orients
human life above all else, is the face of another person. For Levinas,
Cassirer has it right when he looks for the origin of meaning in the
realm of human agency. But to ground meaning in the cultural
productions of societies leaves one trapped in the morass of relativism.
Heidegger was right, Levinas says, to look for the ground of meaning
in something that transcends the human production of symbols, but
to make human action subservient to the impersonal is a mistake of
historic magnitude. Neither Cassirer's humanism nor Heidegger's post-
metaphysical naturalism is able to provide any grounding for ethics.
According to Levinas, this is a scandal. For him, the face comes first.
The moral priority of the other person ruptures the symbol-forming
faculty and provides the transcendent ground for all human action.
As individuals, we are, before all else, responsible. But this relationship
is mutual, it is social. The priority of responsibility is the result of the
mutuality of two vulnerabilities come face to face. Vulnerability to the
other is the ground of compassion, which has priority over all else.

Martin Heidegger was arguably the most important philosopher
of the 20th century, in terms of the far-reaching effect that his work
has had both on those who are sympathetic to his approach and those
who are not. His anti-humanism can elicit a sense of exhilarating
freedom. Hannah Arendt commented that one can feel in his work
the winds that blew through the Greece of the Pre-Socratics. There is
attraction in a release from the claustrophobic sphere of merely human
concerns, with all the inevitable contradictions, confusions, and despair.
Both the scientist and the "poet of Being" are able to escape for a time
from the tangles, complexities, and pains of human life while they are
in the service of some higher cause. And yet such naturalisms can breed
monsters. From a Darwinian point of view, there is no reason
whatsoever to oppose the extinction of the human species, which is,
after all, only one among millions of others, and which will in any
case be replaced in the long run by a competitor. I know people who
seriously propose that we step aside to let our own creation, the
computer, step forward to continue the ascent to some future
apotheosis of Artificial Intelligence. And then, of course, there is the
infamous history of Heidegger himself. This great thinker, and there

is no question whatsoever of his stature as a philosophic mind of the very highest order, this man who, less than two years after the liberation of Auschwitz, could write that "man himself does not matter," was for a time himself a member of the National Socialist Party. He served a brief tenure as rector of the University of Freiburg, lending his considerable prestige to the regime, before he realized that the Nazi political program did not presage the dawn of the greatness of the spirit that he had hoped for. And with one wholly inadequate exception, he never, in all his voluminous body of work, until his death in 1976, spoke or wrote of the Holocaust.[40]

Whether an adequate ethics can be erected with Heidegger's philosophy as its base is the subject of debate. But it does seem that naturalism, whether scientific or post-metaphysical, in its relentless focus on the *non-human*, risks providing cover for a blindness to the dangers of the *inhuman* and the demonic. However, as Levinas clearly saw, humanism is itself not without problems. There is evident in Cassirer's vast written work, as there was in the man himself, a profound humanity and a dedication to the moral imperatives of human life and culture. And yet his philosophy lacks a means of breaking out of the sphere of human symbolization and we are left with the problems of moral and cultural relativism. Levinas's own brand of humanism appeals to a kind of transcendence, but one which is human rather than non-human. The face of the other ruptures the net of symbolization. A humanism without transcendence, however noble in its aspirations, cannot deliver on the promise of moral grounding.

It is here that we may find a connection to Henry Corbin and his theology of the Angel Holy Spirit. For Corbin too finds the necessity of a rupture—a rupture also caused by an encounter with a face. But for Corbin it is the encounter with the face of the Angel. It may happen, for instance, that when we reach the limits of rational understanding, we begin to see the essential motivations of our thoughts as they have arisen from beyond our conscious and rational faculties. He writes:

> ... [I]t is not very often that the philosopher attains such a consciousness of his effort that the rational constructions in which his thought was projected finally show him their connection with his inmost self, so that the secret motivations of which he himself was not yet conscious when he projected his system lie revealed. This revelation marks a rupture of plane in the course of his inner life and meditations. The doctrines

that he has elaborated scientifically prove to be the setting for
his most personal adventure. The lofty constructions of conscious
thought become blurred in the rays not of a twilight but rather
of a dawn, from which figures always foreboded, awaited, and
loved rise into view.[41]

The figures of which he speaks are the figures of the Angels—the
Heavenly Twin who is the Angel Holy Spirit. This encounter is here
described as the end result of long philosophical contemplation. There
are, to be sure, other ways of becoming conscious, but as the Sufis say,
"To know yourself is to know your Lord." The angelic vision is a vision
of the celestial Self. To meet the Angel of the Face is to encounter
transcendence personified and to be transformed by the experience.

For Levinas, the rupture and the face are not mystical. He finds
the possibility of rupture in everyday life, rather than in a rarefied and
private mystical experience. And yet something transcendent must
underwrite the rupture caused by the moral imperative presented by
the face of another person. If we are reducible to historical contingency
and the laws of physics, there can be no rupture. If we are the
mouthpieces for the playing out of the destiny of Being, there may be
rupture of human categories, but it will not be through the moral call
of a person. It is the Angel Holy Spirit that provides the condition for
the possibility of the rupture of plane that is manifested by the moral
call of the person whom I encounter. I do not think there is any
contradiction in finding something mystical and esoteric in the
profoundly individual experience of really seeing another person and
feeling the moral claim that shatters the patterns of complacency and
automatism that structure the routines of daily life.

And for Corbin, too, ethics is central. In the long battle between
the forces of Light and Darkness, our responsibility is clear: the bond
must be maintained between the fallen self and the figure of the
Angel—they are bound together in a pact of spiritual chivalry. The
idea of the connection between the soul and its personal Guide in
Heaven stretches from the Zoroastrian Fravarti, through the Angels
in the Old Testament, to the Holy Spirit in the New, and the Man of
Light and the Hidden Imam in Islam. This theme provides the
possibility of the unification of the Abrahamic faiths in a single
collective task and destiny. This spiritual bond, says Corbin, is *the*
ethical category *par excellence*.[42] Without it there is no access to the

divine, to the *mundus imaginalis*. Then there can be no rupture whatsoever, neither due to the Angelic face, nor to the face of the human other. We will either be trapped in the realm of merely human symbols or be cast adrift in the winds of an indifferent universe.

Within the Angel

Corbin insists that spiritual realities are not accessible to the literal senses, which perceive only public objects in historical time. But this is a potentially dangerous stance and we should take care in interpreting his meaning. It is by claiming special access to knowledge and power that institutional spiritual hierarchies are justified. But for Corbin it is just the esoteric nature of spiritual truth that makes such ecclesial mediation between the individual and the Angel both superfluous and dangerous. Properly speaking, "esoteric" refers to a mode of being that is individual and individuating. In this sense, it is indeed "hidden"—it signifies something inherently inaccessible to others. There need be nothing undemocratic about it at all—all of us have potential access to knowledge of ourselves that is accessible to no one but ourselves. An esoteric community is a communion of true individuals, not a mob in possession of a single common Truth. But more than this, the individuating revelation of the Angel Holy Spirit does not unveil a Truth at all—not a dogma or a law or a fact, not any kind of knowledge that can be used to control, dominate, or comprehend the world or anyone in it. The meeting with the Angel is a release, an opening towards a life in sympathy with the world and its inhabitants. It is an initiation into a form of life dedicated to the transmutation of idols into icons. And idols are not only to be found in the outer world. More importantly, we are all idolators of ourselves. The meeting with the Angel points the way towards an emptying and opening out of the habitual self-centered human life to one of compassion and active love. This is the esoteric meaning of the Passion of Christ, of the self-emptying God become man—the Angel summons us to our true self, which is not an object, not an ego, not any kind of *thing*, but an opening and a process of continual undoing.

The figure of the Angel suggests a synthesis of the compassion for others that humanism stresses and the feeling of liberation from the narrow confines of the ego that is one attraction of naturalism. The iconic life to which the Angel calls us is a more-than-human humanism and opens a path to what the Sufis call the pacified soul, or the soul of tranquility.[43] The spiritual combat of Sufism has as its goal the transformation of the natural soul into the soul of tranquility. But Corbin tells us that this pacification is no motionless quietism. There is no end to the path—the soul is caught up in a never-ending process of transformation and unveiling of spiritual realities. The Angel is the Guide and the archetypal hermeneut, whose function is to reveal the inner meaning of the revealed Word and the spiritual face of every being. The path the Angel opens in a process of what Corbin calls perpetual hermeneutics. There is no limit to theophanies. The soul finds its paradoxical tranquility in a state of motion towards the Divine. The Return of the pacified soul is an eternal progression towards the figure of the Angel, and this passion is itself the soul's proper Home. It is a process of individuation by means of the transformation of the possessive, "imperialist" soul as we turn toward the Face of the Angel. But to begin on this path, we need to know what the turn toward this face is like. We have to take care not to conceive of the turn toward the Angel too literally.

The Angel cannot be understood in anthropomorphic terms alone. The Heavenly Twin is the personification of a process of perception and a way of feeling. The cosmic function of angelophanies is to open our senses to the fullness of being beyond the confines of the material world of secular history. But this need not be mystical in an otherworldly sense. I think we are deceived if we let Corbin's powerful mystical sensibilities blind us to the immediate realities of the world that his thought opens to us. Whenever we feel wonder at the beauty and mystery of the world, it is due to this aspect of the Angel. The most creative scientists are awake to the world this way. Many poets and artists live in the constant presence of the Angel. This reminds us that to live in the neighborhood of the Divine is not easy. Living in the tension between the human and the transcendent can be an agony. This cosmic aspect of the Angelic presence is its transhuman Face.

Corbin speaks often of the process of *interiorization* as a central operation of the creative imagination. Literal realities must be appropriated by the soul and seen as it were from within. But this is not an ego activity, and the world does not get internalized into *me*. In fact, the experience is just the opposite—I get externalized into the world. Suddenly, the world opens and the barriers fall away. This is the goal of contemplation, and it takes place whenever our inner lives open to the space of the Temple. There is latent within us a sacred space—a Temenos or Temple. Of this image Corbin writes:

> I would say that the virtue of the *Imago Templi* lies in making us be *within ourselves outside ourselves*. For we must not confuse introspection, introversion, with contemplation: there is no *contemplation* without the Temple.[44]

When we are in the Temple the world is alive and so are we. This Temple is the place where the personification of nature occurs, as it does in alchemy and astrology. But this is not naturalism—it is not a submersion of the human in Nature. Naturalism of any sort is incapable of comprehending the particularity of the individual person. The personification of nature in alchemy and astrology when they are properly understood is inherently and essentially individual and individuating. It cannot involve the imposition of rules and laws from outside, but is rather the revelation of the Kingdom that unfolds within the place of the Temple.

There is something powerfully transhuman in this cosmic Face of the divine. It is the Face of the sublime—the *mysterium tremendum*—and it is not without danger. In the Islamic tradition, the Names of God fall into two grand categories, the Names of Majesty and the Names of Beauty. The cosmic Face of the Angel is the Face of Majesty. It is not inhuman, as is the demonic, but it is trans-human, and far beyond the scope of our understanding.

The other Face of the Angel *is* more anthropomorphic: the Face of Beauty. But it is not the figure of the Angel that is the object of anthropomorphosis—it is us. At the root of the Abrahamic religions is the intuition that we are made in the image of the Lord. Only in secular society is it assumed that the relation runs the other way. The Angel as a Person is a face of beauty, and makes possible an encounter with another person so powerful as to rupture the fabric of social life.

But how are we to make ourselves susceptible to this rupture? How do we learn to see this face? Can one prepare for breaking the bonds of social life with all its habits, rules, norms, and expectations? It is difficult to imagine being in a constant state of receptivity to the sheer particular humanity of others *as individuals*. You couldn't even walk down the street, let alone get anything *done*. Such a form of life in anything like a pure form, if it were possible at all, could exist only in a small group, and even then, perhaps only transiently. A small group of people coming together, perhaps for a shared meal, to be in company with friends, for no worldly purpose but praise for the blessings of life and love and the glory of being with each other. Something like a family, something like a kind of church. This, I think, is the way esotericists unite.

But to be able to be with each other in this way requires an asceticism based on the renunciation of selfishness and requiring constant and focused attention. We have to be able really to be with other people, and this requires something very difficult indeed—we have to be able to listen. In order to make our way in the world with anything like efficiency and ease, we can't possibly deal with real people—it is too demanding, too time consuming, too painful. So we wear a mask that we can hide behind and that helps guide our behavior and make it predictable—psychologists call this mask our *persona*. We may have many, and, mostly unconsciously, we behave as if all others are wearing them too—and they are. So, to grease the wheels of social interaction, we all behave toward one another on the basis of a limited set of scripts that make it possible for us to interact without really paying much attention. We all come with lots of labels, and we habitually read the labels hanging on everybody else and we behave accordingly. But even worse, and entirely unconsciously, we put masks of our own making on other people, over the ones they put on themselves. These masks that we throw out ourselves are known to psychologists as projections. These projections, of course, come from us, and they show us our own interior face reflected in the faces of others, so that mostly we only ever encounter ourselves. And projections are not inert or innocuous, but are soaked with emotional power. This phenomenon of projection explains the universal fact that what we despise most in others is something deeply hidden inside ourselves. Among all the faces in this confusing theater of masks and projections that we call society, it is not easy to find any real people. To rupture this web of psychosocial interaction, we have to begin by seeking the open place that lies behind the masks and projections. That would be to begin the search for the Angel.

Intimations of the Angel open us to transcendence, to what Corbin and many others have called the vertical dimension of things. But the topologies of higher and lower do not begin to capture the phenomenology of these spaces. We are speaking of what the 17th-century Shi'ite theologian Mulla Sadra called the "intensification of being." Applications of this concept are not restricted to the extravagances of a few mystics. Minimally, it allows us to understand how impoverished our metaphysics has become. For example, we commonly speak of "human behavior"—our children's behavior, our own behavior, of social behavior, economic behavior, ethical behavior. "Behavior" is something we can understand, modify, correct, and control. It is one of those powerful leveling words that make us believe we are speaking about a single kind of phenomenon and thus mask the nature of reality. Things that "behave" can exist only as the kind of beings that *can* behave—and these, I would argue, are material objects having one single kind of *being*. I can, I suppose, imagine the sense in the term "economic behavior" so long as we regard humans as simply "consumers" of 'goods"—that is, all the stuff of materialist economics. But properly speaking, a term such as "ethical behavior" is an oxymoron. Moral categories simply don't apply to the kind of beings that "behave." Individuals behave only when they are not acting as persons, but rather as automatons. The fact that a human being *can* act as a machine, but also as a parent, a lover, a poet, a judge, and indeed, a mystic, is evidence of the reality of a variety of different modes of existence. That there is some kind of hierarchy of these states, though not simply one-dimensional, is the result of the reality of the intensification of being and the ontological plenitude opened to us by the Angel.

The perpetual hermeneutic to which Corbin calls us is a continual re-interpretation of the face the world presents to us; it can lead towards the Open Face of the Angel. It is an unfolding of the closed and defensive ego, a kind of relaxation into the gift of Creation. This hermeneutic is the primary means of revealing and opening us to other modes of being—to the process of intensification of our own being, of our own open, generous, giving personhood. This spiritual journey has a straightforward analog in the psychological process known as "withdrawing projections." Becoming conscious in the sense that Corbin describes as essential in the quest for the Angel requires absolutely that we discover these projections and so begin to unveil our own true face and the true face of the other simultaneously. Projections are rather like idols, and projection is a form of idolatry. We do not exactly worship our projections, but we do assume unquestioningly that they are true because they seem so powerful, so obvious, so objective. But in fact they come from us—they are the beam in our own eye that Jesus said we must remove before we can begin to judge anyone else. The process of coming to understand that these apparent certainties about the world and the people we know in fact belong to us and originate in our own psyche is one of the most difficult in human experience, and is the slow work of many years. It is, I have come to think, in fact perpetual. Some readers may be familiar with the scene in C. S. Lewis's *Chronicles of Narnia* in which Eustace Scrubb, whose self-centered nastiness has turned him into a dragon, has his skins peeled away one after another, as if they were the layers of an onion, by Aslan, the Lion, the Christ-figure in the story.[45] This is an extremely painful process and is, I think, part of what Corbin is referring to when he says that the passage through the Darkness "is a terrifying and painful experience, for it ruins and destroys all the patencies and norms on which the natural man lived and depended— a true 'descent into hell,' the hell of the unconscious."[46] As we begin to discover that what we had assumed about ourselves, other people, and the world as a whole is not in fact the Truth of things, we may become less driven by the search for Truth, more comfortable with not-knowing, less driven by emotion and more able to feel, more able to listen to the other human persons in our lives, and indeed to the quiet promptings of the Angel coming from our deepest self. And so we may come to encounter persons in their mysterious individuality— and these innumerable faces of beauty are each a finite aspect of the face of God.

Peeling away our illusions in this way is one path towards the pacified soul, freed from the angers and passions of the disoriented life. It is a painful and difficult reinterpretation of reality—a true hermeneutic that results in a new way of being in the world, a new mode of presence. It is a means of spiritual transformation essential to the process of becoming the unique individual we are destined to be. The withdrawal of projections, then, is a double process of anthropomorphosis: we are slowly freed to become more human, closer to our own Angel, and at the same time, the figures of the Angels of others become clearer to us in the faces of other people, whom we are more and more able to see truly.

The Prophetic Function of Beauty

And so it is that a hermeneutic ability to see through and re-interpret what we take to be the obvious facts about others and ourselves can transform our perceptions and our mode of presence in the world. This difficult work of becoming conscious is most important, perhaps, with regard to those we love. Corbin has written a great deal about the meaning of human love. Imaginative prayer and love, which have much in common, are the supreme means through which we have direct contact with the divine. The relationships among the persons involved are complex and call for some careful deliberation. For in this scheme, there are several entities actively engaged—the lower soul of the two lovers, the pacified soul of each, the Angel of each, and indeed, Love itself. Making this account more complex is the fact that Corbin's mystical Islamic sources do not distinguish between two forms of love that Christians have come to consider separate: the love we call *eros* and the love known since the times of the New Testament as *agapé*.

In the mystical theology that Corbin describes for us, the vision of the Angel is a revelation of divine Love and Beauty. The beauty of the Divine can manifest only in the form of creatures. Whenever we encounter a being of beauty we are seeing the Beauty of the transcendent Lord. Human beauty is not opposed to divine beauty. Corbin wants to avoid any hint of an ascetical Christian moralism that would deny divine meaning to human love or to the sensuous beauties of creation. The experience of love is profoundly sacramental. It is the sacred occasion at which Flesh is made holy and the means by which the opposition between Spirit and Matter is abolished. Corbin says:

> In place of the negative connection that we habitually understand between Christian asceticism and the Greek consciousness of beauty, it is necessary to speak here of a valorization that confers a prophetic function on beauty.[47]

Beauty is the essential divine attribute, and human love leads to the vision of the unique Lord who is the Angel. Such a love is purified of all merely carnal, possessive instincts, all utilitarian ends, all obsessions and neurotic "needs." Such a chaste love is an ecstasy before the revelation of divine beauty in a being of beauty, a *theophany*. At the limit of this experience of love is the experience of Divine Unity: the Divine being is simultaneously the Loved, the Lover, and the Love itself.[48]

The phenomenon of theophany should be clearly distinguished from that of incarnation. Corbin rejects the Christian theology of the

Incarnation, which places God in Christ, once and for all, in historical time. The dogma of the Incarnation has fatally obscured the true relation between Spirit and Matter and has effected between them a schism that has had profoundly destructive consequences for Western societies. The Christ that Corbin would have us imagine is the Christ of the Cross of Light as described in the apocryphal Acts of John. The true Christ is the Angel Christos, the same figure who is the Angel Holy Spirit, whose image is unique for each of us. But the "image" of the Divine is no phantasm—it is the appearance of that which is truly real. Rather than a dualist opposition between Spirit and Matter, this theology posits what the great medieval Persian mystic Ruzbihan Baqli calls *iltibas*, or "ambiguity," for which Corbin uses the Latin term *amphibole*.[49] The Latin suggests a motion in both directions, and Corbin uses it to imply affinities with *symbole*, whose root meaning is to "throw together." Both terms stand opposed to their opposite, the *diabolic*, which acts to separate and "throw apart."[50] There is no theophany without a moment of *amphibole*. If we can accept this, we will need neither the safety of "literal faith" nor the seeming certainty of sensory facts. The spiritual and the material are mutually interdependent, and the *amphibole* that characterizes all of creation is nothing other than the interpenetration of the sensible and the supra-sensible. The mystical verification of prophetic religion requires the perception of the prophetic meaning of beauty. Beauty is the essential divine attribute and God is the source and reality of love. The sacrament of love can be profaned, and the union of Matter and Spirit in the beauty of Flesh destroyed both by sexual self-indulgence and the ascetic rejection of the divine origin of human beauty.

The amphibolic structure of creation is the result of the fact that every creature is both God and Not-God. At each stage in the hierarchy of creation, when the creatures contemplate the Light that gives them life, they are both different from and identical to that glory. In order to see, they must be other than God, and yet it is from God that they have their very being—for they are nothing, they have nothing, in themselves. This is their radical poverty. Insofar as they are viewed in their difference from God, they seem self-subsistent, and so they run the risk of becoming idols, which are Veils of the divinity. And yet they are the organs by which God contemplates Himself, and so are not other than He. This tension between the vision of creatures as self-subsistent Idols and as Icons of the Divine Light is known as the

Test of the Veils. This spiritual challenge requires that we not become trapped by the self-subsistent, literal face of any being, that we not idolize it but rather see in it the Face of God. Sym-bolic vision depends on the knowledge that both invisible and visible are one; amphi-bolic perception sees with both eyes, the eyes of flesh *and* the eyes of fire; dia-bolic vision throws apart the spiritual and the material and sees only idols everywhere.

Though all creatures shine with Beauty, it is in the human form that this divine glory is most manifest. We are created in the image of God. The secret is to turn neither away from human beauty, nor towards it. It is possible to learn to live in the tension, the ambiguity, between the visible and the invisible. It is possible not to betray the dignity of the human creature and yet to acknowledge, and experience through it, its theophanic essence. The lover is caught in perpetual oscillation between the sensible, visible beauty, and the invisible of the visible that draws us onwards.

The more general problem, in traditional philosophical terms, is the relationship between an apophatic and a cataphatic approach to God. It is not a question of sacrificing one or the other. It is in the tension between them that the soul finds its paradoxical tranquility. Corbin says that it is the theophanic vision that makes it possible to taste the savor and the tranquility of divine love in human love. It is not a question of perception at the level of the sensible world, but of imaginative sensations at the level of the intermediary world of the *mundus imaginalis*. This explains the *amphibole* of the human image, which both *is* and *is not* a sensory image. The sensory experience of the visible and the audible has a double meaning, since it reveals the invisible and the inaudible. This is the theophanic function of the beauty of creation. The beauty of creatures is always apprehended in a form appropriate to the heart of one's own love. The secret of theophanic perception is that it corresponds to the spiritual capacity of the visionary. This seeming multiplicity of the Divine Face may contradict the dogma of the Unity of the Divine, but it is the very revelation of the esoteric unity. God can never be an Object, but is rather the active Subject of the acts of spiritual perception by which the creatures come to know Him. This is the grand paradox of monotheism: the multiplicity of the One and the identity of the Many.

The supreme paradox is that ultimate unity can be attained only by means of the intimate duality of love. The esoteric unity can be understood, lived, and realized only in the experience of love. It is human love that gives access to this unity, because human love is the only experience that can, at its limit, make present the unity of love, lover, and beloved.

This vision of the prophetic meaning of love and beauty stands in total opposition to those ascetics for whom human love is a trap and an obstacle to the experience of the divine. Such an asceticism is a complete inversion of the real meaning of the dia-bolic, since to view beauty and love as obstacles to the divine is truly to throw apart the visible and the invisible. For Corbin, here lies the originality of Iranian Sufism. It expresses an individual ethic, both heroic and secret, a spiritual chivalry based upon the knowledge that it is only through human love that one is able to read the outlines of divine love. One must become initiated into a spiritual hermeneutics, an exegesis of human love that reveals it as a prophetic text. And because Beauty is the source of this text, its discovery is a prophetic action. The lover is thus the partner of the prophet. The message of beauty is a prophetic message: it is an invitation to pass from the human figure, who is the literal text, the place of sensory love, to the truth of love, the esoteric meaning of this text. The Beloved is metamorphosed by the adoration of the Lover, whose love is not a temptation to be overcome but a call to a sublimation of this love, which grants access to the esoteric unity of Love, Lover, and Beloved. This partnership between the prophet and the lover provides the context for the idea of the bond of chivalry between the human being and the Angel, which is, Corbin says, *the* ethical category *par excellence.*

The interior pilgrimage is replete with the torments of "having and not-having." The relationship between human, physical love and divine love is subtle and easily misread. Corbin and his mystical sources tell us that the lover must be purified of all sensual weakness in order to be firm in the path towards spiritual love. Any *purely* carnal appetite must be eliminated. Yet it is not a question of opposing carnality with a brutal and negative "monastic asceticism." While the dangers of idolatry are very real, if we are to transmute the idolatry of physical need into the iconic act of mutual giving, we cannot turn away from the lover entirely. But we are needy creatures and hold too tightly to the human lover. Idolatry may take the form of carnal obsession and the blind appetites of the lower soul. Or it may manifest as a childish dependency on a person, whom we cannot release into his or her own freedom. The impersonal matter of the carnal body is to be transmuted into *flesh*, through which alone a personal presence, human *or* divine, can manifest. The soul can find its Orient in the perpetual motion of having and not having that is the ambiguity of love. Corbin says that th sensory and the suprasensory are but correlative aspects of one and the same *Eros*, and it is the path of mystic love to transform the lower into the higher.

This mystical vision of the meaning of human love, stirring as it is, applies only to certain intense forms of human love. It has no obvious connection to those less passionate forms of human caring and compassion that are so much a part of our everyday lives. Corbin's vision of love is of divine *Eros*. But there are o..ter forms of love, other ways of seeing the human beauty in another person that are more grounded in caring and compassion and moral obligation than in romantic passion. These forms of love are what Christianity calls *agapé*. I think the two are complementary, not contradictory, but they are very different. It seems to me that we can accept Corbin's vision, but we need to expand its range. All beings of light, all human beings, contain the spark of Divine beauty, and so this vision applies to every human encounter and not just to the intensities of the love that Corbin portrays. And *agapé* is not a lower form of *eros*, but a different manifestation of the Face of the Lord. The experience of the caring, active love for another can help us to guard against the dangers that erotic love brings in its wake. Corbin does warn of these, but his cautions are easily missed if we are in thrall to the myth of romantic love.

Denis de Rougemont set forth a typology of love that is helpful in this context. In his now classic work, *Love in the Western World*, first published in 1939, de Rougemont proposed a thesis about the rise of romantic love in Western culture that has been both controversial and widely influential.[51] He regarded the development of typically Western attitudes to love and to God to be the result of a tension between the "divine delirium" of the Greek *eros*, and the active, incarnate love, or *agapé* of the New Testament. It is worth quoting at length a passage that touches on the elements most pertinent to a critical view of Corbin's account of love. De Rougemont writes:

> Eros is complete Desire, luminous Aspiration, the primitive
> religious soaring carried to its loftiest pitch, to the extreme

> exigency of purity which is also the extreme exigency of Unity.
> But absolute unity must be the negation of the present human
> being in his suffering multiplicity. The supreme soaring of desire
> ends in non-desire. The erotic process introduces into life an
> element foreign to the diastole and systole of sexual attraction—
> a desire that never relapses, that nothing can satisfy, that even
> rejects and flees the temptation to obtain its fulfillment in the
> world, because its demand is to embrace no less than the All. It
> is *infinite transcendence*, man's rise to his God. And this rise is
> *without return.*[52]

The one-way flight of transcendence is characteristically combined
with powerful dualisms between spirit and matter, God and the Devil,
Light and Darkness in the cultures that gave rise to the basic religion
of Europe. These "Eastern" religions, among them Manicheanism,
which is central in de Rougemont's story, tend to emphasize the flight
from this world and a "unitive" form of mysticism in which the
individual seeks impersonal immersion—and so, effectively,
annihilation—in the divine.

In the West, this Erotic passion became entangled with the
archetypal figures of Woman, giving rise to the troubadours, Arthurian
romance, and the ideal of romantic love, which is so characteristic of
Western culture from the 12th century on. In the West,

> Eros has taken the guise of Woman, and symbolizes both the
> other world and the nostalgia which makes us despise earthly
> joys. But the symbol is ambiguous, since it tends to mingle
> sexual attraction with *eternal* desire. ... [The figure of Woman]
> stirred up a yearning for what lies beyond embodied forms.
> Although she was beautiful and desirable for herself, it was her
> nature to vanish.[53]

The idealization of Woman and the unstable erotic passion of romantic
love are incompatible with mature, lasting relationships between actual
men and women. De Rougemont argues that it is this tension that
provides much of the frenzied energy of the modern West.

The source of the energy is the tension between the transcendence
of *eros* and the incarnate immanence of *agapé*. The typically Western
attitude, as de Rougemont sees it, is based upon the experience of a
fundamental abyss between God and man, an attitude that makes
unitive mysticisms highly heretical. The orthodox mysticism of the
West is *epithalamian*, and the highest human experience of God is

conceived of as a mystical marriage, based upon the *descent* of grace from above. The basic dynamic of *agapé* is communal, a relationship of individuals. "The symbol of Love is no longer the infinite *passion* of a soul in quest of light, but the *marriage* of Christ and the Church."[54] Because of the Incarnation, we are engaged not in a dynamic out of the world, but rather in the beginning of a new life *here*, where we can begin to love the other person "as he or she really is." The passionate love of *eros* is uncontrolled, a divine influx that explodes the personality and overthrows our will. It is impersonal in that it is both out of the lover's control and not concerned with the other person *as an individual*. It is not "active love." De Rougemont says, "*To be in love* is not necessarily *to love*. To be in love is a state; to love, an act. A state is suffered or undergone; but an act has to be decided upon."[55] Marriage, divine or human, is an instance of active love.

> The imperative, "Love God and thy neighbor as thyself", creates structures of active relations. The imperative "Be in love!" would be devoid of meaning; or, if it could be obeyed, would deprive man of his freedom.[56]

In the later editions of this book, de Rougemont stresses that it was never his intention to suggest that passion and marriage are incompatible. He argues for the necessary tension of opposites. Once the tensions were recognized, "there had to be a decision to live out their drama and choose to experience their ever-changing and surprising tension."[57] De Rougemont proposes that we seek to enact a third form of love, one that helps to reconcile the visions presented by Corbin and Levinas. De Rougemont writes:

> If it is true that passion seeks the Inaccessible, and if it is true that the Other as such remains the best-defended mystery in the eyes of a demanding love—could Eros and Agape not join in a paradoxical alliance at the very heart of an accepted marriage? Is not every *Other* the Inaccessible ...? This search for the Angel, which is the mystery of the Other, exciting both Eros and Agape—might it not be a third form of love, similar to the mysticisms of spiritual marriage?[58]

If this is true of the marriage bond, it applies equally, it seems to me, to the ethical bond established by the rupture that the call of the other person makes on my life. Both encounters call me out of myself in a responsibility to the other; this is the immanent mirror of the chivalric bond with the face of the divine, a bond that is the basis of all ethical action.

One further question to consider, if we are to adopt Corbin's Angelic theology, is this: When we encounter the mystery and depth of another person, whose Angel are we seeing? In Manichean legend, when, after death, on the Bridge to the other world, the soul meets its Angel in the figure of a beautiful woman, she says, "I am thyself." De Rougemont disparagingly calls this "mystical narcissism."[59] (Elsewhere, he wonders what form the Angel of a woman takes.)[60] The Angel Holy Spirit is, as we know, in each case unique. Corbin's mystic

> knows that he is the eye with which God contemplates himself;
> that he himself, in his being, is the witness by which God
> witnesses himself, the revelation by which the Hidden Treasure
> reveals itself to itself.[61]

But Corbin and his Islamic spiritual masters are absolved from charges of both implicit narcissism and the annihilation of the person in Divine Union by two facts. The person of the Angel is infinite and iconic—that is, the succession of transcendences never stops. The meeting with the Angel does not set up a closed system, in which the soul finds itself contemplating its own beauty in a transcendently self-satisfied manner. The lower soul, the soul that seeks such narcissistic pleasure, is in fact annihilated. The true self opens upwards, and forever. Corbin says:

> Personal survival cannot ... be thought of as purely and simply
> prolonging the status of the human condition, the "acquired
> dispositions." The latter doubtless concern what we call the
> "personality." But ... the essential person in its posthumous
> becoming and in its immortality perhaps immeasurably
> transcends the "personality" of so-and-so son of so-and-so.[62]

Secondly, there is no Union "in general," for each soul is forever on its way towards its perfect individuation. The next world is full of individuated beings, each one unique. The world of Light is populated with Angelic beings who are the Guides for the beings below. These are the Fravartis, "those who have chosen" to aid in the battle with Ahriman, the Prince of Darkness. Each soul

> has its Fravarti. What they announce to earthly beings is ... an
> essentially dual structure that gives to each one a heavenly
> archetype or Angel, whose earthly counterpart he is.[63]

> It is this fravarti which gives its true dimension to the person. The human person is only a person by virtue of this celestial dimension, archetypal, angelic, which is the celestial pole without which the terrestrial pole of his human dimension is completely *depolarized* in vagabondage and perdition.[64]

This figure of the Holy Spirit, the homologue of the Christ of the Cross of Light, is in no way a mirror of the fallen human self, such as would be the case if this were narcissism. On the contrary, it is the face of the Lord that the soul encounters, without which we are lost.

> It is not in the power of a human being to destroy his celestial Idea; but it is in his power to betray it, to separate himself from it, to have, at the entrance to the Chinvat Bridge, nothing face to face with him but the abominable and demonic caricature of his "I" delivered over to himself without a heavenly sponsor.[65]

But then, what of the Otherness of the other person, in whose face alone we can see the Lord? Corbin tells us that we are seeing their Angel in the only way we can see the Divine—in a form appropriate to the heart of our own love. It is necessary to be open to them. And the bond between us is one of unity in duality—this is the amphibole. But then, too, there is the third thing, the Love that unites. It is the Love that is the gift of the Holy Spirit, the rupture that sets us outside of social rules and norms. At the summit of human love, where the union of the partners occurs, we find the Angelic dimension of two human persons united by the common love that they share. This paradoxical unity in diversity reflects what Christians know as the doctrine of the Trinity.

This is where the Test of the Veils occurs—in the finding and the not-finding, in the acceptance and rejection of responsibility, in the failures and successes of human love of every sort. In this vision, where Love and Prophecy are united, the call to love and the call to justice are two faces of the same summons. We succeed and fail in turns, but we cannot refuse the responsibility.

Any search for the Angel is a search for both the divine face and the human. We, who are enthralled by these imaginal worlds that Corbin has opened up, must take care not to turn the Angel into an Idol. It is an easy error to fall prey to. Seeking the Angel for Her own sake before we are spiritually ready can become an escapist and narcissistic endeavor. This is one of the perennial dangers of mysticism, and it reminds us why Masters are necessary. Hidden knowledge, esoteric knowledge, is hidden not because only an Elite may know it, but because one must have reached a certain stage of maturity to understand it. Such maturity makes it possible to live with ambiguity. The tension is not easy to bear. Corbin tells us that the Angel is accessible only through a being of beauty whom we love. The Test of the Veils is to see the two faces of the divine simultaneously—neither reducing the Divine to the human, nor effacing the human through the overwhelming power of the Divine. This is the true meaning of the paradox of the Incarnation. The true Incarnation is not the established dogma that once and for all time God became man in the person of Jesus the Christ. The Angel, the figure of the Paraclete, the Holy Spirit of the New Testament, makes possible the incarnation *in the flesh* of every one of us every time we love. The Angel provides the possibility of the person, but we must provide the incarnation—this is a job that cannot be done for us. When the Fathers of the early Church were struggling with the hermeneutics of the nascent doctrine of the God-Man, they took the wrong path. The truth is more ecumenical, more difficult, and more individual. The amphibolic structure of human beings means that we exist most truly in this interworld, poised between counterbalanced idols. On the one hand is the impersonal obsession with the desires of the body or the entrapment of others in the prisons of our own needs. On the other is the figure of an Angel, who would save us from the complex and difficult tasks of active love and justice. Either of these idolatries destroys the possibility of knowing and becoming incarnate flesh. It is the tension that establishes the imaginal world—it is this tension that provides the energy for the simultaneous Descent and Return that constitutes the living reality of Creation. When I love another, it is my Angel and theirs that ensure that we see and are seen as icons, not idols. If the bond with the Angel is broken, then Flesh becomes matter, love becomes passion, and the world falls into chaos.

The bond of active love between two persons is the ethical bond that underlies all others. Because the Angels too must be active for such a bond to form, the bond also establishes the incarnate reality of the *imaginal* world. Incarnation is an event of the soul and the exercise of *imaginatio vera* is an ethical act. True imagination is distinguished from fantasy by at least these signs: it frees the ego from obsessive desires; it brings to consciousness projected illusions and so transforms idols; and, as a consequence, it increases our capacity to love, to perceive the iconic face of the beloved.

An Addressable Thou

One reason the figure of the Angel is to be approached with caution is that understood impersonally, by the rational mind alone, it may seem to offer a transcendent escape from the utter vulnerability required for personal love. But love is personal, intimate, and particular and can be understood only esoterically. It is the chief means by which the esoteric is known. This Personal face of the Angel opens us to the sympathy that allows us to feel compassion. And this brings us to tears. Speaking of the life of active love, the Eastern Orthodox theologian Olivier Clément says:

> Make no mistake, setting out on this path means becoming vulnerable to all the pain of the world. If we did not know that Christ had shed his blood on the cross and uttered his cry of unimaginable despair, we should be crushed beyond recall. Everyone who relinquishes the security of a sleepwalking existence is sooner or later mortally wounded by the world's suffering. But because God became man and took his suffering on himself, the way of vulnerability and death becomes for us resurrection.[66]

In the quest for the *mundus imaginalis,* there can be no denial of darkness. Michael Auping has put it succinctly in discussing the work of Anselm Kiefer, an artist who has struggled to look deeply into the depths of evil. Auping says, "The idea of Heaven can elevate us only if it can carry the weight of history."[67] One can, of course, reject the idea of Heaven altogether. One possible response to the anguish of human suffering is some form of naturalism. We can take refuge in the impersonalism of technology or the quest for scientific truth, and in the naturalist's hope that, as Heidegger said, "man does not matter." But such an inhumanism signals the final destruction of the prophetic tradition and the disappearance of the person, and it threatens to institute a politics of power and domination unimpeded by any principled opposition.

The challenge of humanism requires understanding that the Angel is our partner in the battle for the soul of the world. The stakes are high and the adversaries powerful. As Corbin says, we must pass through the Hell of the unconscious in ourselves, *and* we must engage with the forces of darkness in the world, for "the God of Light has need of the aid of all his followers," because the menace of nihilism is terrifying.[68] This makes the search for the dual faces of the Angel, both human and divine, the primary ethical task. We have to search for the reality of persons in a world where this reality is in question. Science tells us there is no such thing. And the demonic horrors of the last century seem to prove the point. In dark times, the essential thing is that there *be* persons. Where the connections between the earthly and the Divine are severed, we have to re-forge them.

And what of those of us who do not have Clément's faith in the Christ of the Cross or in the Covenant with the God of Abraham or in the mercy and compassion of Allah? What of those for whom the way of vulnerability and death brings no resurrection? How will these bear the pain of compassion? And even for those who do hold on to remnants of faith, what can they do if the bond of chivalry, of love, is broken? How does one re-imagine a world that seems to have been abandoned by God, and in which our very humanity seems at risk? What power is at our disposal that is adequate to this task?

Corbin's answer is that we have the Creative Imagination. And in the tradition for which he speaks, the primary way in which this power is expressed is through the Word, through language. In one of his last letters from prison, before he was murdered by the Nazis, the Lutheran pastor Dietrich Bonhoeffer wrote:

> It is not for us to prophesy the day (though the day will come) when men will once more be called so to utter the word of God that the world will be changed and renewed by it. It will be a new language, perhaps quite non-religious, but liberating and redeeming—as was Jesus' language; it will shock people and yet overcome them by its power ....[69]

This language of which he speaks is, by definition, poetic language. It is through the imaginative power of language that we may best be able to seek that Angel, who confronts us intimately in the face of another person. And in our dark time, there are only a few poets able to shoulder the burden. Among them, the life and work of Paul Celan are worth particular attention. His writings can tell us something profound about the nature of the creative imagination and the search for the Person in our time.

The work of this Romanian Jewish poet, survivor of the death camps, confronts the triple catastrophe issuing from "that which happened": the opening of the chasm between God and man, the destruction of the bond between human beings, and the near annihilation of the imaginative power of language. Everything was lost to the Jews in the Shoah. But not quite everything. Celan says that only one thing remained in the midst of all the losses: language. Out of this remainder, what can be made? What power can this language have in the poem? Poems, he says, are "making toward something."

> Toward what? Toward something standing open, occupiable, perhaps towards an addressable Thou, toward an addressable reality.[70]

In a time when the very idea of a personal God seems to be a blasphemy against the reality of human suffering, the poet's task is to search for an addressable Thou, an addressable reality. Addressable, *personal*. This is the form that the search for the face of the other may take in our time. Naturalism and humanism come together in this search for an addressable reality, in the more-than-human reality that we seek— perhaps this *is* the battle for the soul of the world in our time.[71]

Celan chose to write in German and to fight against the near destruction of language by the "terrible silencing" of human speech that was the Holocaust. Language itself was deformed and degraded by the fascist horror, and by the insidious hollowing out that the modern technological world requires of it.[72] Celan says that language

> ... had to pass through its own answerlessness, pass through frightful muting, pass through the thousand darknesses of deathbringing speech. It passed through and brought back no words for that which happened; yet it passed through this happening. Passed through and could come to light again, "enriched" by all this.
>
> In this language I have sought ... to write poems: so as to speak, to orient myself, to find out where I was and where I meant to go, to sketch out reality for myself.[73]

There can be no more powerful and poignant statement of the desperate human need for the potential of the creative imagination to forge the bond between persons and so to sketch out reality, to show each of us where we are and where we are meant to go. I think we should hear the echoes of Celan's voice, and the silenced voices of those for whom he speaks, when we contemplate the words of Henry Corbin. Corbin was a prophet of the imagination, and of the living Word which is its embodiment. Corbin's unifying vision of the Abrahamic tradition allows us to see that this is the same Word that Celan worked to rescue from the inhuman impersonality of the modern world by sketching out a reality, an addressable reality, for himself, and for us. This task falls most heavily on poets, who, as Corbin has said, are those to whom the Imagination was entrusted when it was rejected by philosophy and the positive sciences. But we need to be fully aware of the responsibility that we all bear in this battle for the soul of the world. Our pact with the Angel requires us to be active participants in this fundamental human and humanizing act of creative imagination. Bonhoeffer foresaw a new language, redeeming and liberating; poetic language at its finest is on the way toward something—it is an orientation. Words risen from death and from the near death of language are perhaps the form that prayer takes in our time—a time in which the world has been stripped of the category of the Person. The search for an addressable Thou, at once human and divine, is precisely the act of prayer. For, as Corbin tells us once again, "prayer is not a request for something: it is the expression of a mode of being, a means of existing and of *causing to exist*"[74]—of causing the Angel to exist, our own Angel, whose image conforms to the state of our soul, and through whose action alone we can see the *person* in the incarnate flesh of another human being. The search for a language truly adequate to address another person *is* prayer, which, as Corbin insists, is "the supreme act of the Creative Imagination."

CHAPTER SEVEN

A Personal Story

A philosophy can only be formulated by a soul which has
found itself; may those who have found be of service to those
who are searching!

—Henry Corbin[1]

It has slowly dawned on me over the last two decades that I am a
very religious person. I did not know this, and did not understand
my chronic disorientation as a symptom of this ignorance. I spent
my undergraduate years reading ostensibly secular Western
philosophy, and then, later on, many more years studying aggressively
secular Western science. It just won't do. Everything important is
simply left out, and it eventually clamors to get in by the back door.
The categories and forms of religious life and thought are inescapable
if we are to have any chance of living human lives in this mysterious
world. So I should become some sort of Christian—I certainly have
the pedigree. I discovered not long ago that the "cheet" in Cheetham
(one of the very few roots in English that survive from the Old Celtic)
signifies "woods." The "ham" is Anglo-Saxon, meaning "homestead"
or "dwelling." So, Cheetham means something like "woods dwelling,"
a circumstance I am rather happy about, since I actually live in one.
My paternal great-grandfather was from Lancashire and my mother's
family is Irish. Over the years, I have been attracted to Buddhism, and
for a time I thought Sufism might do. But my family tree is Christian
and it is growing in pagan Celtic soil. Yet the Protestantism to which

I was intermittently subjected as a child felt entirely dead—all old maids, darkness, and musty pews. I was never exposed to anything like the heart of the tradition.

Now I know rather more, and have discovered some of the astonishing things hidden there. My years of trying to understand the theology of Henry Corbin have brought me from time to time very close to calling myself a Christian. Perhaps I am one. If so, I am Christian in a sense that has little in common with what most people understand by the term. I cannot help but feel that we stand near the end of a tradition and must imagine it anew. The history of the religions of the Book is filled with horrors and betrayals, violence and hatred, contradictions and absurdities, and one can only wonder whether this history is now coming to some catastrophic, even apocalyptic conclusion. And yet I have come to understand that there is at the heart of the tradition something elusive and so precious that it cannot be abandoned. It cannot wholly disappear if human beings, human *persons*, are to have a future. I owe most the modest awareness I have of this hidden treasure to Henry Corbin.

I can remember clearly the first time I read James Hillman's 1979 Eranos Lecture. It begins with this vivid and moving encomium:

> You who have been privileged at some time during his long life to have attended a lecture by Henry Corbin have been present at a manifestation of the thought of the heart. You have been witness to its creative imagination, its theophanic power of bringing the divine face into visibility. You will also know in your hearts that the communication of the thought of the heart proceeds in that fashion of which he was master, as a *récit*, an account of the imaginal life as a journey among imaginal essences, an account of the essential. In him imagination was utterly presence. One was in the presence of imagination itself, that imagination in which and by which the spirit moves from the heart towards all origination.[2]

Since the hour in which I first read these words, I have been variously puzzled, thrilled, enchanted, obsessed, sometimes even repelled, but always haunted by my imagination of Corbin the man and of his work. He has never since been very far from my mind. My relation to his books is not academic. It is certainly not scholarly, since I know so little of the subjects of which he was such a masterful scholar. Although I never knew him, my relation to him and to his work is personal. My unfolding of Corbin's work, my explanation of it to myself, is a story I have been telling and re-telling to myself for many years now. What it means to have a personal story is the topic of this final chapter.

Corbin was a master of the thought of the heart, of the *récit*, the visionary recital. The *récit*, as he intends the term, is the archetypal personal narrative. The ability to recite the Event of the soul guarantees each of us our individuality. The paradigmatic examples for Corbin are the recitals of Suhrawardi and Avicenna. The collected works of both masters, he tells us, have this in common:

> ... [S]ide by side with extremely solid systematic works, they both contain a cycle of brief spiritual romances, narratives of inner initiations, marking a rupture of plane with the level on which the patencies successively acquired by theoretical expositions are interconnected.[3]

The accounts bear such titles as "The Recital of the Bird," "The Recital of Occidental Exile," "The Crimson Archangel," and "The Reverberation of Gabriel's Wing."[4] These narrative dramas are not subsidiary to the philosophical systems, they are not allegorical tales meant to "illustrate" or explain. Quite the reverse. They perhaps bear the same relation to a "story" as an icon does to a picture. They are in fact the culmination, the summit of the imaginative universe that the rational mind has produced. Corbin says, "By substituting a dramaturgy for cosmology, the recitals guarantee the genuineness of this universe."[5] The recital is not a fiction, it is not an objective history of facts, and it is not an allegory, in which personified figures stand for abstract concepts. It is "the soul's own story ... the soul can tell it only in the first person."[6] In a complete inversion of the scheme of things commonly taken for granted, the truth of a philosophical system, of a general description of things as produced by the rational intellect, is verified and guaranteed by its transformation into a personal Event of an individual soul. This is a staggering rejection of everything that secular rationality presupposes about reality. The foundation of all things is not matter, or energy, or mind, or even some vaguely general idea of Spirit—it is nothing general or abstract or "universal." At the heart of reality is the Person—concrete and individual, and "for each one unique." The Event of the soul that the recital displays turns the schema of the world inside out:

> For the Event carries us to the utmost limit of the World; at
> this limit, the cosmos yields before the soul, it can no longer
> escape being interiorized into the soul, being *integrated* with
> it. This is the phase at which the psychic energy performs
> the transmutation of the text—here the "cosmic text"—into
> a constellation of symbols. ... What the soul suddenly
> visualizes is its *own* archetypal Image, that Image whose
> imprint it simultaneously bears within it, projects, and
> recognizes outside itself.[7]

The summit of contemplation is an exegesis of the text of the world,
and the recitals are the track of the exodus of the soul from
estrangement and disorientation and towards its Orient, its celestial
origin—towards the Face of the Angel. The hermeneutic of the world
"permits the perception of beings and things in their person—that is,
as thought by a person,"[8] and such perception encounters beings in
the Orient, in the realm of the Angel. This is the meaning of Oriental
philosophy, and any philosophy worth pursuing *must* be Oriental. The
goal of philosophical contemplation is finally to bring us Home—to
ourselves and to a world come alive with meaning and with the light
of Heaven. In one of his last essays, Corbin writes that "Orientals" in
the spiritual and metaphysical sense are now dispersed and hidden
throughout all the countries of the world, but were they to respond
to the call, "Orientals of the world, Unite!" they might then together
provide an answer to the question: "What is the use of philosophers?"[9]

The goal of the spiritual Quest is to make the world our own. We
are called to be Home Makers. This vision of spiritual ecology neither
makes of our species a Lord of Creation nor reduces us to an
epiphenomenon of the impersonal forces of nature. The world needs
us. Unless we become persons, and so escape from exile in impersonal
anonymity, the world remains an Object, "unthought by a person"
and neither God nor Things can exist.

Corbin has shown us that theophanic prayer is *creative*—it is a
means of bringing into being the Angelic countenance whose Face
is actualized by *our* act of Imagination—and precisely because this
Imagination is a divine, personal, personified gift, whose powers
only *we* can exercise. Corbin presents Suhrawardi and Ibn 'Arabi,
among others in the Islamic tradition, as masters of this power,

but he is also fond of citing passages from the *Cherubinic Wanderer*, by the 17th-century Christian mystic Angelus Silesius. Here, too, we find the idea of companionship and "chivalry" bonding the Angel and the human soul to whom it corresponds. Corbin quotes these striking verses:

> I know God cannot live one instant without Me:
> If I should come to naught, needs must He cease to be.[10]

> God's need of me, my need of God,
> Are equal in degree.
> He helps to bear my being up
> And I help Him to be.[11]

> Naught is but I and Thou. Were there nor Thou nor I,
> Then God is no more God, and Heaven falls from the sky.[12]

Corbin's theology of Angelic mediation makes these remarkable lines more transparent than they can be for traditional monotheism. It is not the "God of Gods" who does not exist without us—it is the Lord, the Angel Holy Spirit, whose fiery face opens out into a myriad theophanies to bring to light the diversity of creation. We are necessary partners in this creative, intimate, personal relationship with the transcendent. The bond with the Angel requires everything from us. The Annunciation is not an event in history—it is a call:

> "Hail Mary!" so thou greetedst Her:
> Yet, Gabriel, what doth this avail
> To me, unless thou likewise come
> And greet me with the self-same "Hail!"

> I must be Mary and myself
> Give birth to God, would I possess
> —Nor can I otherwise—God's gift
> Of everlasting Happiness.[13]

The power of the creative imagination, the gift of Gabriel, the Angel Holy Spirit, enables each of us, if we consent, to give birth to the Angel, whose grace allows us to see all the world as an icon. For we give birth not only to God, but to the world itself, transfigured in the light of a personal vision.

There is, Corbin tells us, a remarkable concordance between certain mystical Islamic accounts of the Angel and the late poetry of Rainer Maria Rilke. Rilke himself believed that his vision of the Angel had more in common with the Angels of Islam than with those of the Christianity he knew. Rilke's mystic vision implies a cosmology that denies any gulf between Heaven and Earth—the two are, rather, continuous. It is, I think, this fundamental intuition that makes his work so important for Corbin. Corbin, whose knowledge of German theology, philosophy, and literature was astonishingly broad and deep, believed that Rilke's *Elegies* "formulate exactly, literally" the central themes of the Islamic mystic vision, which he so passionately defended.[14] Corbin quotes from a well-known letter Rilke wrote a year before his death: "… [O]ur task is to stamp this provisional, perishing earth into ourselves so deeply, so painfully and passionately, that its being may rise again, 'invisibly,' in us." We must perform a transfiguration of the visible into the invisible. It is in the figure of the Angel, which is central to the *Elegies*, that this transformation appears already accomplished. Rilke wrote:

> The Angel of the *Elegies* is the being who vouches for the recognition in the invisible of a higher order of reality.—Hence "terrible" to us, because we, its lovers and transformers, do still cling to the visible.—All the worlds of the universe are plunging into the invisible as into their next deepest reality. … We are these transformers of the earth; our entire existence, the flights and plunges of our love, everything qualifies us for this task (besides which there is, essentially, no other).[15]

Corbin says that this is precisely the view of Avicenna, Suhrawardi, Mulla Sadra, and Ibn 'Arabi. In language that mirrors Rilke's, the 20th-century Shi'ite theologian Mohammad Hosayn Tabataba'i said that the function of the Gnostic in this world is to be the workshop for the production of the invisible, the transcendent.[16] The imagination in us provides the necessary meeting place between this world and the Divine. Corbin tells of a Shi'ite tradition which holds that the blood of Imam Hosayn, Prince of Martyrs, must remain suspended forever between Heaven and Earth, for if it were ever to fall, the world would come to an end.[17] The Angel allows us to perceive all things as suspended between Heaven and Earth in the *mundus imaginalis*. The Imagination establishes the reality of the "meeting place of the two seas," where Moses meets Khidr, the Verdant One.[18]

Rilke perceived all this with startling clarity and sensitivity. The world needs us. Things need us. In the Ninth Elegy he asks: "... [W]hy then / have to be human ...?" The answer: "... [B]ecause *truly* being here is so much; because everything here / apparently needs us ...."[19] We are here just in order to be fully *present* and so, in Corbin's words, able to live "a life in sympathy with beings, capable of giving a transcendent dimension to their being, to their beauty ...."[20] The angelic function of beings is to liberate us for transcendence.[21] Things are here only if they are more than here.[22] Our function is to ensure that this transcendent dimension is opened so that we, and the beings of the earth, can be fully *incarnate*, wholly *present*. The paradox is that the simple presence and individuality of any being are granted only by virtue of transcendence. The intensity of existence is measured on a vertical scale. The vertical dimension is the dimension of the Person.

Rilke says: "Perhaps we are *here* in order to say: house, / bridge, fountain, gate, pitcher, fruit-tree, window,"[23] but we must speak these names with more intensity than the things could ever *have* by themselves. The language of imagination is the bridge between the worlds. The divine and the ordinary are fused into one reality in which the immanent and the transcendent are part of a continuous whole. This whole is "mystical" in some sense, but at the same time "purely earthly, deeply earthly, blissfully earthly."[24] It is Imagination that opens out the ordinary into its "widest orbit," into the realm of the imaginal. It is language that guarantees the existence of these Things: "*Here* is the time for the *sayable, here* is its homeland. /... [T]he Things that we might experience are vanishing, for / what crowds them out ... is an imageless act.[25] It is the imagination, actualized by a person in an imaginal act of personification, that can stand against the imageless act that threatens the existence of Things. The essence of the speech and the witness that exalts the imagination and reveals the angelic function of the things of the world is *praise*: "Praise this world to the angel ... /... Tell him of Things. He will stand astonished ...."[26]

We are imagining animals. We live and die by the imagination. I was a couple years shy of my fortieth birthday when the power and all-encompassing grandeur of the Imagination began to force itself upon me. I had, by then, been a member of one academic institution or another for many years, either as a student or a teacher. Bewildered by my discovery, I was astonished by the balance of power between the humanities and the sciences. Why don't the professors of literature and poetry *talk* about the power of the imagination? And why do the sciences get all the money? Part of the answer, at least in the world of academia, is that there are precious few people who can accept the stark reality of William Carlos Williams's claim that "men die miserably every day,"[27] starved of the sustenance that poetry can provide.

The space in which we live is opened by imagination. The stories we tell ourselves *are* our lives. Much of modern culture is based on a perversion and betrayal of this precious gift. It is still within our power to resist the erasure of individuality that the modern world threatens to make permanent. Corbin's life-work is a prolonged and profound meditation on the power of the image in the service of the individual. A primary means by which imagination becomes embodied is language— through poetry and story. The visionary recital is an exalted species of the same genus as the humblest poem, novel, play, or story. And all are conscious manifestations of the continuous current of imaginings that are the substance of conscious and unconscious life. It is the great challenge of human existence to find an entry into that stream of life— to find the myth we are living, the story that is ours, the world that is ours to inhabit. It lies within the power of the *récit* to make us *present* and open to Things, to other people, and to the Angel. It is the Lost Speech of the spirit, without which we are doomed. Suhrawardi says that the Spirit is a being of Light that shines in the mind. When this light wavers, we are consumed with melancholy and the energies of life wane.[28] Yet even such despair is a form of presence, transformable, redeemable by the imagination. All of life can be transformed in the presence of the figure of the unknowable Guide, who offers the possibility of seeking the true self, the Face we had before the world was made. The supreme paradox is this: you cannot know who you are without opening to the darkness of the unknown. You cannot be present in the fullest sense until you are able to follow the fearsome Angel leading you on into the dark. You must learn to live with the unknown in front of you,[29] "because truly being here is so much."[30]

> Friend, this is enough. If you want to read more,
> Go and be yourself the letter and the spirit.
>
> *Angelus Silesius*[31]

I have seen the cross hanging in the cool church vaults. At times it resembles a split-second snapshot of something moving at tremendous speed.

—Tomas Tranströmer

Notes

CHAPTER ONE: MYSTICAL POVERTY AND THE THEORY OF THE WORLD

1. In Christian Jambet, ed., *Henry Corbin*, Cahier de l'Herne, no. 39, Consacré à Henry Corbin (Paris : Ed. de l'Herne, 1981), pp. 62-3; italics in original.
2. Henry Corbin, *The Man of Light in Iranian Sufism*, trans. N. Pearson (New Lebanon, NY: Omega Publications, 1994), p. 112.
3. *Ibid.*, pp. 112-113; italics in original.
4. Henry Corbin, "De la théologie apophatique comme antidote du nihilisme," in *Le Paradoxe du Monothèisme* (Paris: Ed. de l'Herne/Le Livre de Poche, 1981), pp. 194-5.
5. 1 Kings 19:12 (RSV).
6. The Qur'an 50:16.
7. Henry Corbin, "De la théologie apophatique," p. 203.
8. These are the words of Ivan Illich. See David Cayley, *Rivers North of the Future: The Testament of Ivan Illich as told to David Cayley* (Toronto: Anansi Press, 2005), p. 63.
9. C. G. Jung, *The Collected Works of C. G. Jung*, trans. R. F. C. Hull, vol. 6 (Princeton, NJ: Princeton University Press, 1971), para. 62. (Hereafter abbreviated to *CW*, followed by volume number and paragraph number.)
10. Henry Corbin, *Spiritual Body & Celestial Earth: From Mazdean Iran to Shi'ite Iran*, trans. N. Pearson, Bollingen Series XCI: 2 (Princeton, NJ: Princeton University Press, 1977), p. 81. (5th Printing, 1989, with *Prelude to the Second Edition: Towards a Chart of the Imaginal.*)
11. *Peri psyche* III, 8, 432b20.
12. Plotinus, *The Ennead* VI, 5, 7, trans. Stephen MacKenna (Burdett, NY: Larson Publications, 1992).
13 Michael Sells, *Mystical Languages of Unsaying* (Chicago, IL: University of Chicago Press, 1994), esp. pp. 17-32.
14. Eric Partridge, *Origins: A Short Dictionary of English Etymology* (New York: Macmillan, 1966), s.v. *theater*.
15. John Deck, *Nature, Contemplation and the One: A Study in the Philosophy of Plotinus* (Toronto: University of Toronto Press, 1967).

16. Henry Corbin, *Alone with the Alone: Creative Imagination in the Sufism of Ibn 'Arabi*, trans. R. Manheim, Bollingen Series XCI (Princeton, NJ: Princeton University Press, 1997), pp. 115-116. (Hereafter referred to as *Creative Imagination*.)

17. Corbin, *Man of Light*, p. 16.

18. See David Abram, *The Spell of the Sensuous: Perception and Language in a More-Than-Human World* (New York: Pantheon, 1996), p. 130.

19. Quoted in Corbin, *Creative Imagination*, p. 106.

20. Quoted in Corbin, *Spiritual Body*, p. 146.

21. Corbin, *En Islam Iranienne: Aspects spirituels et philosophiques, Tome I: Le shi'isme duodècemain* (Paris: Gallimard, Bib. des Idees, 1971), p. 141; italics in original.

22. Corbin, *Creative Imagination*, p. xxviii.

23. Rainer Maria Rilke, *Selected Poems of Rainer Maria Rilke: A Translation from the German and Commentary by Robert Bly* (New York: Harper and Row, 1981), p. 107.

24. Seyyed Hossein Nasr, "Oral Transmission and the Book in Islamic Education: The Spoken and the Written Word," in *The Book in the Islamic World: The Written Word and Communication in the Middle East*, ed. George N. Atiyeh (Albany, NY: State University of New York Press, 1995), p. 57.

25. Michael Sells, *Approaching the Qu'ran: The Early Revelations* (Ashland, OR: White Cloud Press, 1999), p. 11.

26. William Chittick, *The Self-Disclosure of God: Principles of Ibn 'Arabi's Cosmology* (Albany, NY: State University of New York Press, 1998), p. xxxvi.

27. *Ibid.*, p. xxxv.

28. *Ibid.*, pp. xxxvi-xxxvii.

29. See Daphne Hampson, "Luther on the Self: A Feminist Critique," in *Feminist Theology: A Reader*, ed. Ann Loades (Louisville, KY: Westminster/John Knox Press, 1990), pp. 215-225.

30. Ivan Illich, *In the Vineyard of the Text: A Commentary to Hugh's Didascalicon* (Chicago, IL: University of Chicago Press, 1993), p. 11.

31. See *Spell of the Sensuous*.

32. George Steiner, *Real Presences* (Chicago, IL: University of Chicago Press, 1989), p. 69.

33. *Ibid.*, 142.

34. *Ibid.*, 198.

35. *Ibid.*, 226.

36. Quoted in Corbin, *Creative Imagination*, p. 106.

37. Corbin, *En Islam Iranien: Aspects spirituels et philosophiques, Tome IV: L'Ecole d'Ispahan - L'Ecole Shaykhie - Le Douzieme Imam* (Paris: Gallimard, Bibliothéque des Idees, 1973), p. 168.

38. Corbin, *Creative Imagination*, p. 248; italics in original.

39. *Ibid.*, p. 249.

CHAPTER TWO: THE UN-REFUSED FEAST

1. See Tom Cheetham, *The World Turned Inside Out: Henry Corbin and Islamic Mysticism* (New Orleans, LA: Spring Journal Books, 2003) and *Green Man, Earth Angel: The Prophetic Tradition and the Battle for the Soul of the World*, with an Introduction by Robert Sardello, SUNY Series in the Western Esoteric Tradition (Albany, NY: State University of New York Press, 2005).

2. Henry Corbin, "L'Initiation Ismaèlienne ou l'Esoterisme et le Verbe," in *L'Homme et Son Ange: Initiation et Chevalerie Spirituelle* (Paris: Fayard, 1983), p. 81.

3. See Henry Corbin, *Creative Imagination in the Sufism of Ibn 'Arabi*, trans. R. Manheim, Bollingen Series XCI (Princeton, NJ: Princeton University Press, 1969), pp. 53ff.

4. *Ibid.*, p. 55.

5. Henry Corbin, "The Configuration of the Temple of the Ka'bah as the Secret of the Spiritual Life," in *Temple and Contemplation*, trans. P. Sherrard and L. Sherrard (London: Kegan Paul International, 1986), p. 189.

6. Letter 550, in *The Letters of D. H. Lawrence, Vol. 5*, ed. James T. Boulton and Lindeth Vasey (Cambridge, UK: Cambridge University Press, 1989).

7. Henry Corbin, "Theophanies and Mirros: Idols or Icons?" trans. Jane Pratt and A. K. Donohue, *Spring 1983*, p. 2.

8. Luke 14:16-18.

9. Henry Corbin, *The Man of Light in Iranian Sufism*, trans. N. Pearson (New Lebanon, NY: Omega Publications, 1994), p. 145. See Matt. 22:2-10; Luke 14:16-24.

10. Luke 14:33.

11. Margaret Miles, *Carnal Knowing: Female Nakedness and Religious Meaning in the Christian West* (Boston, MA: Beacon Press, 1989), p. 185.

12. C. G. Jung, *The Collected Works of C. G.* Jung, trans. R. F. C. Hull, vol. 14 (Princeton, NJ: Princeton University Press, 1970), para. 531. (Hereafter abbreviated to *CW* followed by volume number and paragraph number.

13. Corbin, *Creative Imagination*, p. 80.

14. Henry Corbin, *Avicenna and the Visionary Recital*, trans. Willard Trask, Bollingen Series LXVI (Princeton, NJ: Princeton University Press, 1960), pp. 92-93.

15. Corbin, *Creative Imagination*, p. 244.

16. Jung *CW* 14, § 512.

17. *Ibid.*

18. Corbin, *Man of Light*, pp. 65-66.

19. Walt Whitman, "Song of Myself," ll. 669-71, in *Leaves of Grass*, ed. Sculley Bradley and Harold Blodgett (New York: W. W. Norton, 1973), p. 59.

20. Walt Whitman, "A Song of the Rolling Earth," ll. 1-4, 7, 10, in *Leaves of*

Grass, ed. Sculley Bradley and Harold Blodgett (New York: W. W. Norton, 1973), p. 219.

21. *Ibid.*, ll. 91-92, p. 223.
22. Quoted in Margaret Miles, *Fullness of Life: Historical Foundations for a New Asceticism* (Philadelphia, PA: Westminster Press, 1981), p. 9. Bishop Serapion (d. 365-70) was Bishop of Thmuis in the Nile delta.
23. William Blake, *The Poems of William Blake*, ed. W. H. Stevenson (New York: W. W. Norton, 1971), Plate 5: From an engraving of the Laocoön.
24. Seyyed Hossein Nasr, *Ideals and Realities of Islam* (London: Allen & Unwin, 1966), quoted in Norman O. Brown, "The Apocalypse of Islam," in *Apocalypse &/or Metamorphosis* (Berkeley, CA: University of California Press, 1991), p. 90.
25. *Ibid.*
26. Robert Inchausti, "Introduction," in Thomas Merton, *Seeds*, ed. and intro. Robert Inchausti (Boston, MA: Shambhala Publications, 2002), p. xi.
27. *Ibid.*, pp. 76-77.
28. Thomas Merton, *Thomas Merton: Spiritual Master—The Essential Writings*, ed. Lawrence S. Cunningham (New York: Paulist Press, 1992), p. 426.
29. Corbin, *Man of Light*, p. 117.
30. Ivan Illich, "The Rebirth of Epimethean Man," in *Deschooling Society* (New York: Harper, 1971), p. 152. Also helpful is Lee Hoinacki, "Reading Ivan Illich," in *The Challenges of Ivan Illich: A Collective Reflection*, ed. Lee Hoinacki and Carl Mitcham (Albany, NY: State University of New York Press, 2002), pp. 1-7.
31. Dôgen, *Moon in a Dewdrop: Writings of Zen Master Dôgen*, ed. Kazuaki Tanahashi (New York: North Point, 1985), p. 69.
32. Olivier Clément, *On Being Human: A Spiritual Anthropology* (New York: New City Press, 2000), p. 32; italics in original.
33. *Ibid.*, p. 160.
34. Olivier Clément, *The Roots of Christian Mysticism: Texts From the Patristic Era with Commentary* (London: New City Press, 1993), p. 211.
35. *Ibid.*, p. 215.
36. *Ibid.*, p. 222.

CHAPTER THREE: THE FLAME OF THINGS

1. Henry Corbin, "L'Initiation Ismaèlienne ou l'Esoterisme et le Verbe," in *L'Homme et Son Ange: Initiation et Chevalerie Spirituelle* (Paris: Fayard, 1983), p. 81.
2. Henry Corbin, *Spiritual Body & Celestial Earth: From Mazdean Iran to Shi'ite Iran*, trans. N. Pearson, Bollingen Series XCI: 2 (Princeton, NJ: Princeton University Press, 1977), p. xvii. (5th Printing, 1989, with *Prelude to the Second Edition: Towards a Chart of the Imaginal*.)

3. 1 Cor. 13 (RSV).
4. Henry Corbin, "The Configuration of the Temple of the Ka'bah as the Secret of the Spiritual Life," in *Temple and Contemplation*, trans. P. Sherrard and L. Sherrard (London: Kegan Paul International, 1986), p. 189.
5. Genesis 3:9. (RSV)
6. Henry Corbin, *The Man of Light in Iranian Sufism*, trans. N. Pearson (New Lebanon, NY: Omega Publications, 1994), p. 1; italics in original.
7. Quoted in Jerome Rothenberg and Pierre Joris, *Poems for the Millennium, Volume 2: From Postwar to Millennium* (Berkeley, CA: University of California Press, 1998), p. 798.
8. Olivier Clément, *The Roots of Christian Mysticism: Texts From the Patristic Era with Commentary* (London: New City Press, 1993), p. 135.
9. *Ibid.*, p. 135.
10. *Ibid.*, p. 167.
11. Henry Corbin, "Theophanies and Mirrors: Idols or Icons?" trans. Jane Pratt and A. K. Donohue, *Spring 1983* (1983): 2.
12. See, for example, Philip Sherrard, *Christianity: Lineaments of a Sacred Tradition* (Brookline, MA: Holy Cross Orthodox Press, 1998), Chapter 6.
13. John Chryssavgis, *In the Heart of the Desert: The Spirituality of the Desert Fathers and Mothers* (Bloomington, IN: World Wisdom, 2003), p. 54.
14. Clément, pp. 130-148.
15. Aidan Kavanagh, *On Liturgical Theology* (Collegeville, MN: The Liturgical Press, 1984), pp. 160-161.
16. Corbin, "Theophanies," p. 2.
17. Kavanagh, p. 4.
18. David Cayley, *Rivers North of the Future: The Testament of Ivan Illich as told to David Cayley* (Toronto: Anansi Press, 2005), p. 119.
19. Thomas Merton, *Seeds*, ed. and intro. Robert Inchausti (Boston, MA: Shambhala Publications, 2002), pp. 91-92.
20. Robert Inchausti, *Thomas Merton's American Prophecy* (Albany, NY: State University of New York Press, 1998), pp. 175-176.
21. Shunryu Suzuki, *Zen Mind, Beginner's Mind* (New York: Weatherhill Inc., 1970), pp. 116-117.
22. Christopher Alexander, *The Nature of Order: An Essay on the Art of Building and the Nature of the Universe—Book One: The Phenomenon of Life* (New York: Oxford University Press, 2001), pp. 212-213.
23. See Paul Evdokimov, *The Art of the Icon: A Theology of Beauty* (Crestwood, NY: St. Vladimir's Seminary Press, 1990), p. 23 and the whole of Ch. 5.
24. Christopher Alexander, *The Nature of Order: An Essay on the Art of Building and the Nature of the Universe—Book Two: The Process of Creating Life* (Berkeley, CA: The Center for Environmental Structure, 2002), p. 494.
25. Gary Snyder, *The Real Work: Interviews and Talks 1964-1979* (New York: New Directions Publishing Corp., 1980), p. 83.

26. See Corbin, *Man of Light*.

27. Roshi Philip Kapleau, *Three Pillars of Zen: Teaching, Practice and Enlightenment*, new ed. (New York: Anchor Books, 1989), p. 126 and note.

28. Suzuki, p. 84.

29. Quoted in Clément, p. 209.

30. Paul Radin, *Primitve Man as Philosopher* (New York: Dover Books, 1957), pp. 246-247.

31. Stanley Diamond, *In Search of the Primitive: A Critique of Civilization* (London: Transaction Books, 1974), p. 196.

32. Kapleau, p. 296.

33. Clément, pp. 228-229.

34. Paul Evdokimov, *Ages of the Spiritual Life* (Crestwood, NY: St. Vladimir's Seminary Press, 1998), p. 110.

35. Evdokimov, pp. 11-12.

36. Henry Corbin, "Eyes of Flesh and Eyes of Fire: Science and Gnosis," *Material for Thought* 8 (1980): 10.

37. Henry Corbin, *Alone with the Alone: Creative Imagination in the Sufism of Ibn 'Arabi*, trans. R. Manheim, Bollingen Series XCI (Princeton, NJ: Princeton University Press, 1997), p. 134.

CHAPTER FOUR: THE CROSS OF LIGHT

1. Pierre Lory has recently discussed aspects of Corbin's life and work in his review of Stephen M. Wasserstrom, *Religion After Religion: Gershom Scholem, Mircea Eliade and Henry Corbin at Eranos* (Princeton, NJ: Princeton University Press, 1999), which presents a highly critical appraisal of Corbin. Lory presented his remarks at *Le 1ère journée Henry Corbin*, 17 December 2005, at the Sorbonne in Paris. The text can be read at the website of the Association of the Friends of Henry and Stella Corbin, www.amiscorbin.com. Also pertinent is Maria E. Subtelny's review of Wasserstrom, "History and Religion: The Fallacy of Metaphysical Questions (A Review Article)," *Iranian Studies* 36, no. 1 (March 2003): 91-101.

2. Henry Corbin,"Divine Epiphany and Spiritual Birth in Ismailian Gnosis," in *Cyclical Time and Ismaili Gnosis*, trans. R. Manheim and J. Morris (London: Kegan Paul International, 1983), p. 64.

3. Good accounts of recent scholarship on these issues can be found in Peter R. Carrell, *Jesus and the Angels: Angelology and the Christology of the Apocalypse of John* (Cambridge, UK: Cambridge University Press, 1997); Crispin H. T. Fletcher-Louis, *Luke Acts: Angels, Christology and Soteriology* (Tübingen: J. C. B. Mohr, 1997); and Darrell D. Hannah, *Michael and Christ: Michael Traditions and Angel Christology in Early Christianity* (Tübingen: Mohr Siebeck, 1999). While Corbin bases a good deal of his

discussion in "Divine Epiphany" on the work of Martin Werner, subsequent scholarship has largely rejected Werner's conclusions. The issues are complex, but according to Hannah, there is nonetheless no doubt that Jewish angelology had an influence on early Christianity, and many scholars place "a great deal of importance on ancient Jewish conceptions and beliefs about angels in the development of early Christology" (Hannah, p. 11).

4. For a very accessible introduction to this early history upon which I have drawn here, see Bart D. Ehrman, *Lost Christianities: The Battles for Scripture and the Faiths We Never Knew* (Oxford, UK: Oxford University Press, 2003). In an indispensable and fascinating treatment of the relation between Judaism and Christianity, Daniel Boyarin, *Border Lines: The Partition of Judeo-Christianity* (Philadelphia, PA: University of Pennsylvania Press, 2004), argues that until the end of the 4th century, "Judaism and Christianity were phenomenologically indistinguishable as entities, not merely in the conventionally accepted sense, that Christianity was a Judaism, but also in the sense that differences that were in the fullness of time to constitute the very basis for the distinction between the 'two religions' ran through and not between the nascent groups of Jesus-following Jews and Jews who did not follow Jesus" (Boyarin, p. 89).

5. For what follows, see Corbin, "Divine Epiphany," pp. 59-61.

6. *Ibid.*, pp. 60-61; italics in original.

7. Acts of John 97-102 in M. R. James, *The Apocryphal New Testament* (Oxford, UK: Clarendon Press, 1950), pp. 254-256.

8. Corbin, "Divine Epiphany," p. 60.

9. Henry Corbin, "Harmonia Abrahamica," preface to Luigi Cirillo and Michel Frémaux, *Évangile de Barnabé: Recherches sur la composition et l'origine* (Paris: Éditions Beauchesne, 1977), p. 14.

10 C. G. Jung, *The Collected Works of C. G. Jung*, trans. R. F. C. Hull, vol. 11 (Princeton, NJ: Princeton University Press, 19), paras. 430-31, quoted in Corbin, "Divine Epiphany," p. 63, n. 9.

11. *Ibid.*, p. 63.

12. *Ibid.*, p. 64.

13. John 14: 6 (RSV).

14. Quoted in Corbin, "Divine Epiphany," p. 66; From Pseudo-Clementine, *Recognitiones* 2, 9, 22.

15. Henry Corbin, "Le paradoxe du monothèisme," in *Le Paradoxe du Monothèisme* (Paris: Ed. de l'Herne/Le Livre de Poche, 1981).

16. Samuel Butler, *Erewhon and Erewhon Revisited* (New York: Modern Library, 1955), p. 367, quoted in Corbin, "Le paradoxe," pp. 57-58.

17. Quoted in Corbin, "Le paradoxe," p. 58.

18. *Ibid.*, p. 59.

19. It seems fairly clear what a docetic interpretation of the transformation of

the consecrated bread and wine would be: each communicant sees what is within his or her ability to see. The Eucharist is an event in the soul, a theophany, and given a cosmology in which matter and spirit are not divided, there is no need to argue about transubstantiation and doctrines of the Real Presence. Corbin speaks fondly of the private liturgies developed by certain Shi'ites [*Alone with the Alone: Creative Imagination in the Sufism of Ibn 'Arabi*, trans. R. Manheim, Bollingen Series XCI (Princeton, NJ: Princeton University Press, 1997), pp. 259 and 372, n. 17. (Hereafter referred to as *Creative Imagination*.)], and his strong, "Protestant" distaste for human intermediaries between God and His faithful is evident in all of his work. The Eucharist must be a "private" affair in this sense. And if one abandons a Christocentric theology, if Christ is not the literal Son of God, upon whom all of History hinges, then the Eucharist cannot be a universal sacrament.

20. See Tom Cheetham, *Green Man, Earth Angel: The Prophetic Tradition and the Battle for the Soul of the World*, with an introduction by Robert Sardello, SUNY Series in the Western Esoteric Tradition (Albany, NY: State University of New York Press, 2005).

21. Genesis 18: 1-8 (NRSV).

22. Corbin, *Creative Imagination*, p. 131.

23. Olivier Clément, *The Roots of Christian Mysticism: Texts From the Patristic Era with Commentary* (London: New City Press, 1993), pp. 379-380.

24. See Ehrman.

25. e. e. cummings, "Advice to Young Poets," in *A Miscellany / Revised*, ed. with introduction and notes by George J. Firmage (New York: October House, 1965), p. 335. I thank Dave Henry for drawing this quote to my attention.

26. See David Cayley, *Rivers North of the Future: The Testament of Ivan Illich as told to David Cayley* (Toronto: Anansi Press, 2005), pp. 208ff.

27. The late work of Maurice Merleau-Ponty is of significance in this context. He came to call "flesh" the relationship that he intuited was the deep structure of the embodied world. David Abram comments that with this term, Merleau-Ponty pointed to "an elemental power that has no name in the entire history of Western philosophy" [*The Spell of the Sensuous: Perception and Language in a More-Than-Human World* (New York: Pantheon Books, 1996), p. 66. While this may well be true of the strictly philosophical tradition, it is not true of the Western theological tradition. See Maurice Merleau-Ponty, *The Visible and the Invisible* (Evanston, IL: Northwestern University Press, 1968).

28. Henry Corbin, "Eyes of Flesh and Eyes of Fire: Science and Gnosis," *Material for Thought* 8 (1980): 5-10.

29. Corbin, *Creative Imagination*, p. 248.

30. Ivan Illich, cited in Cayley, *Ivan Illich: In Conversation* (Concord, Ontario: Anansi Press, 1992), p. 211.
31. *The Catholic Encyclopedia*, s.v. Liturgy.
32. Corbin, *Creative Imagination*, p. 3.

CHAPTER FIVE: TOUCHING GRACE

1. Henry Corbin, "Divine Epiphany and Spiritual Birth in Ismailian Gnosis," in *Cyclical Time and Ismaili Gnosis*, trans. R. Manheim and J. Morris (London: Kegan Paul International, 1983), p. 148.
2.. Andrew Todd and Franco La Cecla, "Ivan Illich," *The Guardian*, December 9, 2002, p. 22.
3. Thomas Quigley, "News Briefs," *Catholic News Service, U.S.*, December 10, 2002.
4. Lee Hoinacki and Carl Mitcham, eds., *The Challenges of Ivan Illich: A Collective Reflection* (Albany, NY: State University of New York Press, 2002), p. 4.
5. Ivan Illich, "The Loss of World and Flesh," trans. by Muska Nagel and Barbara Duden, available online through the *Thinking After Illich* website. In German as "Verlust von Welt und Fleisch," in *Freitag* 51(13). December 2002, s. 18, 1993a, 3.
6. Luke 10: 25-37 (RSV).
7. David Cayley, *Rivers North of the Future. The Testament of Ivan Illich as told to David Cayley* (Toronto: Anansi Press, 2005), p. 30.
8. *Ibid.*, pp. 30-31.
9. See *Ibid.*, p. 237, n. 89.
10. *Ibid.*, p. 29.
11. Quoted in Cayley, from a lecture, "Hospitality and Pain," given in Chicago in 1987.
12. *Ibid.*, p. 29.
13. *Ibid.*, p. 59.
14. 2 Thess. 2: 7.
15. Cayley, p. 59.
16. *Ibid.*, p. 61.
17. *Ibid.*, p. 176.
18. *Ibid.*, p. 177.
19. *Ibid.*, p. 179.
20. *Ibid.*, p. 62.
21. *Ibid.*, p. 178.
22. Henry Corbin, *Alone with the Alone: Creative Imagination in the Sufism of Ibn 'Arabi*, trans. R. Manheim, Bollingen Series XCI (Princeton: Princeton University Press, 1997), p. 134. (Hereafter referred to as *Creative Imagination*.)

23. *Ibid.,* pp. 106-107.
24. *Ibid.,* pp. 290-294.
25. *Ibid.,* p. 134.
26. Henry Corbin, *Avicenna and the Visionary Recital,* trans. W. Trask, Bollingen Series LXVI (Princeton: Princeton University Press, 1960), pp. 116-117.
27. For Corbin, the difference between an idol and an icon lies more in *how* one sees than in *what* one sees. This is why he can say that the entire universe of theophanic forms can become "one immense iconostasis." —"Theophanies and Mirrors: Idols or Icons?" trans. Jane Pratt and A. K. Donohue, *Spring* (1983): 2.
28. On "stuff," see Ivan Illich, *H₂O and the Waters of Forgetfulness: Reflections on the Historicity of Stuff* (Dallas, TX: Dallas Institute of Art and Humanities, 1984).
29. What follows is a condensation of some of the key ideas in a late essay, as yet unpublished, that Illich wrote in collaboration with Barbara Duden, Mother Jerome, O.S.B., and Lee Hoinacki. The essay, entitled "The Scopic Past and the Ethics of the Gaze: A Plea for the Historical Study of Ocular Perception," is accessible at Ivan Illich Archives, Personal website of David Tinapple, 2002, <http://www.davidtinapple.com/illich/1998_scopic_past.PDF>.
30. Alain Besançon, *The Forbidden Image: An Intellectual History of Iconoclasm,* trans. Jane Marie Todd (Chicago, IL: University of Chicago Press, 2000). (In French, 1994).
31. F. Edward Cranz, "The Reorientation of Western Thought c. 1100 AD: The Break with the Ancient Tradition and Its Consequences for Renaissance and Reformation," paper delivered at the Duke University Center for Medieval and Renaissance Studies, March 24, 1982, unpublished. His major essays on this topic have only recently been published in Cranz, *Reorientations of Western Thought from Antiquity to the Renaissanc,* ed. Nancy Streuver (London: W. H. Smith, 2006).
32. Henry Corbin, *En Islam Iranienne: Aspects spirituels et philosophiques, Tome I: Le shi'isme duodècemain* (Paris: Gallimard, Bib. des Idees, 1971), p. 37.
33. Gérard Simon, *Le regard, l'être et l'apparence dans l'optique de l'antiquité* (Paris: Éditions du Seuil, 1988).
34. Quoted in Illich, "Scopic Past," p. 6.
35. Surely this is just the meaning of Merleau-Ponty's (1968) struggles with his own notions of the Chiasm, and the flesh of the world. In the present context, the connection with Corbin can be found in Henry Corbin, *The Man of Light in Iranian Sufism,* trans. N. Pearson (New Lebanon, NY: Omega Publications, 1994), pp. 139-144, where Corbin discusses the physiology of the Man of Light. But Corbin characteristically speaks of the trans-sensory nature of the phenomenon.

36. Illich, "Scopic Past," p. 6.
37. Cayley, p. 136.
38. Ibid., 134.
39. Ibid., 132.
40. Illich, "Scopic Past," p. 6.
41. *Ibid.*, p. 8.
42. *Ibid.*, p. 9. Illich is speaking here of the relatively late work of Peter of Limoges in particular, but this work represents a long tradition.
43. *Ibid.*, p. 10.
44. *Ibid.*, p. 9.
45. *Ibid.*, p. 8.
46. The issue of the active intellect is of more than passing interest because of the central role it plays in Corbin's thought—see Tom Cheetham, *The World Turned Inside Out: Henry Corbin and Islamic Mysticism* (New Orleans. LA: Spring Journal Books, 2003). The medieval doctrines of the active intellect derive from a single passage in Aristotle's *De Anima*, in which Aristotle posits two sorts of soul, one active and one passive. The active soul, or *nous poietikos*, partakes somehow in the divine. These short passages gave rise to fertile speculation, particularly among the Neoplatonists, in medieval thought, and in Islamic philosophy. (There is of course a vast literature on the subject. The interested reader can find a selected bibliography of the argument over Aristotle's own meaning in Victor Caston, "Aristotle's Two Intellects: A Modest Proposal," *Phronesis* 44, no. 3 (1999): 199-227. Franz Brentano, "Nous Poiêtikos: Survey of Earlier Interpretations," in *Essays on Aristotle's De Anima*, ed. M. Nussbaum and A. Rorty (Oxford, UK: Clarendon Press, 1992), pp. 313-41 is also useful as an historical survey. Von Franz provides analysis of and commentary on a text sometimes attributed to Aquinas that treats of the agent intellect, and gives a reading in line with Jung's psychology. See Marie-Louise von Franz, *Aurora Consurgens: A Document Attributed to Thomas Aquinas on the Problem of Opposites in Alchemy*, ed. with a commentary by M.-L. von Franz, trans. R. F. C. Hull and A. S. B. Glover (Torono: Inner City Books, 2000), pp. 166ff. For Corbin, the crucial point is that in the Islamic prophetology of Avicenna and Suhrawardi, this Neoplatonic discussion took a striking turn. The Active Intellect, which for Aristotle is the trace of God, who moves our intellects "as a beloved" as he moves the heavenly spheres (Caston), becomes, for the Illuminationist tradition in Islam, the Angel Gabriel, who is the Angel Holy Spirit, the same figure who is the Paraclete in the Gospel of John, and the Christ of the Cross of Light. Corbin writes, "In the perspective of the Paraclete, the three Abrahamic faiths can come together in the same city-temple" ["The *Imago Templi* in Confrontation with Secular Norms," in *Temple and Contemplation*, trans. P. Sherrard and L. Sherrard (London: Kegan Paul International, 1986), p. 338].

47. Illich, "Scopic Past," p. 16.
48. One of the clearest and most reliable interpreters of Levinas's often difficult work is Richard A. Cohen. See, for example, Richard A. Cohen, *Ethics, Exegesis and Philosophy: Interpretation after Levinas* (Cambridge, UK: Cambridge University Press, 2001); and "Introduction," to Emmanuel Levinas, *Humanism of the Other*, trans. Nidra Poller (Urbana, IL: University of Illinois, 2003).
49. Illich, "Scopic Past," p. 16.
50. *Ibid.*, p. 17.
51. *Ibid.*, p. 6.
52. *Ibid.*, p. 17.
53. Cayley, p. 205.
54. *Ibid.*, p. 207.
55. *Ibid.*
56. *Ibid.*, p. 197.
57. *Ibid.*, p. 207.
58. *Ibid.*, p. 214, my italics.
59. *Ibid.*, p. 80.
60. *Ibid.*, p. 95.
61. *Ibid.*, p. 163.
62. *Ibid.*, p. 101.
63. See his critiques of Averroes in Corbin, *Avicenna*, p. 82 and Corbin, *Creative Imagination,* p. 12.

CHAPTER SIX: WORDS OF THE HEART

1. Henry Corbin, *Spiritual Body & Celestial Earth: From Mazdean Iran to Shi'ite Iran*, trans. N. Pearson, Bollingen Series XCI: 2 (Princeton, NJ: Princeton University Press, 1977), pp. vii-x. (Translation slightly altered.) The 5th printing (1989) included Corbn's *Prelude to the Second Edition: Towards a Chart of the Imaginal*. Many English readers have been puzzled by the fact that the *Prelude to the Second Edition* appeared only with the 5th printing of the English edition.
2. Henry Corbin, *Alone with the Alone: Creative Imagination in the Sufism of Ibn 'Arabi*, trans. R. Manheim, Bollingen Series XCI (Princeton: Princeton University Press, 1997), p. 4. (Hereafter referred to as *Creative Imagination*.)
3. Henry Corbin, "*Mundus Imaginalis* or the Imaginary and the Imaginal," in *Swedenborg and Esoteric Islam*, trans. L. Fox (West Chester, PA: Swedenborg Foundation, 1995), p. 11, italics in original.
4. Corbin, *Creative Imagination*, p. 80.
5. *Ibid.*, p. 248, italics in original.
6. Corbin, "*Mundus Imaginalis,*" p. 20.
7. Denis de Rougemont, "Hérétiques des toutes les religions ...," in *Henry*

Corbin, ed. Christian Jambet, Cahier de l'Herne, no. 39, Consacré à Henry Corbin (Paris: Ed. de l'Herne, 1981), p. 298.

8. *Ibid.*, p. 301.

9. I am not unaware of the dangers of vague and careless appropriations of the term "imaginal." William Chittick [*Imaginal Worlds: Ibn al-'Arabi and the Problem of Religious Diversity* (Albany, NY: State University of New York Press, 1994)] and Christian Jambet [*The Act of Being: The Philosophy of Revelation in Mullâ Sadrâ*, trans. Jeff Fort (New York: Zone Books, 2006)] have echoed Corbin in emphasizing the necessity of understanding the precise genealogy and context that give the term its meaning in Islamic thought. It is important indeed to recognize that the *mundus imaginalis* requires a docetic cosmology quite different from the Incarnationism that forms the context of modern Western theology, philosophy, and science. Jambet cautions that the *imaginal* is profoundly serious. He writes: "The *agent* imagination has a *prophetological* function, a *moral* use, and an *eschatological* role." (p. 285, italics in original). Keeping these cautions in mind, it is, I think, consistent with Corbin's ecumenism that we make the attempt to discover what meaning the Agent Imagination can have for us in the modern world. These essays are "attempts" in that spirit.

10 Henry Corbin, *Avicenna and the Visionary Recital*, trans. W. Trask, Bollingen Series LXVI (Princeton, NJ: Princeton University Press, 1960), p. 159.

11. Henry Corbin, "From the Gnosis of Antiquity to Ismaili Gnosis," in *Cyclical Time & Ismaili Gnosis*, trans. Ralph Manheim and James W. Morris (London: Kegan Paul International, 1983), pp. 192-193.

12. Henry Corbin, *En Islam Iranienne: Aspects spirituels et philosophiques, Tome I: Le shi'isme duodècemain* (Paris: Gallimard, Bibliothéque des Idees, 1971), pp. 26ff.

13. Whether Gnosticism is a particular religion or a group of religions that influenced Judaism and Christianity is a complex question. Corbin does indeed draw, sometimes heavily, on various "Gnostic" texts, but the validity of his general arguments is not affected by the fact that scholars have denied the existence of a single Gnostic "religion." This was never Corbin's central point, and his claim for the universality of *gnosis* has no relation to the existence or non-existence of any particular Gnostic sect. It is true that Corbin's accounts of the emprisonment of the soul in the material world often show considerable sympathy for views that are Gnostic in a narrow sense, but he was not entirely consistent in this. For a discussion of the "Gnostic" religion, see Karen L. King, *What Is Gnosticism?* (Cambridge, MA: Harvard University Press, 2003).

14. For a more detailed account, see Tom Cheetham, *Green Man, Earth Angel: The Prophetic Tradition and the Battle for the Soul of the World*, with an introduction by Robert Sardello, SUNY Series in the Western Esoteric

Tradition (Albany, NY: State University of New York Press, 2005), Ch. 3.

15. Henry Corbin, *The Man of Light in Iranian Sufism*, trans. N. Pearson (New Lebanon, NY: Omega Publications, 1994), p. 47.

16. Corbin, *Spiritual Body*, pp. xviii-xix.

17. For this, see James Hillman, *Re-Visioning Psychology* (New York: Harper & Row, 1975); *A Blue Fire: Selected Writings by James Hillman*, ed. and intro. Thomas Moore (New York: Harper Collins, 1989); *Archetypal Psychology*, Uniform Edition of the Writings of James Hillman. Vol. 1 (Putnam, CT: Spring Publications, 2004).

18. See especially James Hillman, *The Thought of the Heart and the Soul of the World* (Dallas, TX: Spring Publications, 1992).

19. Hillman, *Archetypal Psychology*, p. 45.

20. The original statement of this position is in James Hillman, "Psychology: Monotheistic or Polytheistic?" *Spring 1971* (1971): 193-208.

21. Henry Corbin, "Prefatory Letter" to *The New Polytheism*, by David L. Miller (Dallas, TX: Spring Publications, 1981).

22. Henry Corbin, "Le paradoxe du monothèisme," in *Le Paradoxe du Monothèisme* (Paris: Ed. de l'Herne/Le Livre de Poche, 1981), p. 7.

23. Corbin, *Creative Imagination*, p. 121.

24. Corbin, "Le paradoxe du monothèisme," p. 59.

25. James Hillman, *Kinds of Power: A Guide to Its Intelligent Uses* (New York: Doubleday, 1995), pp. 249-50.

26. James Hillman, "Psychology: Monotheistic or Polytheistic: Twenty Five Years Later," *Spring 60* (1996): 111-125.

27. Hillman, *Archetypal Psychology*, p. 50.

28. James Hillman, "On the Necessity of Abnormal Psychology: Ananke and Athene," in *Facing the Gods*, ed. James Hillman (Irving, TX: Spring Publications, 1980), p. 33, n. 5, italics in original. This paper was originally presented at Eranos in 1974.

29. Corbin, *Creative Imagination*, p. 224.

30. Harold Bloom, *Omens of Millennium: The Gnosis of Angels, Dreams, and Resurrection* (New York: Riverhead Books, 1997). See also: Cheetham, *The World Turned Inside Out* for some brief comments.

31. Harold Bloom, "Preface," *Alone with the Alone: Creative Imagination in the Sufism of Ibn 'Arabi*, by Henry Corbin, trans. R. Manheim, Bollingen Series XCI (Princeton: Princeton University Press, 1997 (Princeton, NJ: Princeton University Press, 1997), p. xiv.

32. *Ibid.*, p. xix.

33. Harold Bloom, *Shakespeare: The Invention of the Human* (New York: Riverhead Books, 1998), p. 15.

34. Ron Rosenbaum, *The Shakespeare Wars: Clashing Scholars, Public Fiascoes, Palace Coups* (New York: Random House, 2006). On Bloom in particular, see Chapter 12.

35. *Ibid.*, p. xvi.

36. Corbin, *Creative Imagination*, p. 67.

37. For an extended treatment of this signal event, see Michael Friedman, *A Parting of the Ways: Carnap, Cassirer and Heidegger* (Chicago, IL: Open Court Publishing Company, 2000).

38. I am indebted to an essay by Richard Cohen for my brief remarks on this encounter between these two seminal thinkers. See Cohen, "Introduction," *Humanism of the Other*, by Emmanuel Levinas, trans. Nidra Poller (Urbana, IL: University of Illinois, 2003).

39. Martin Heidegger, "Letter on Humanism," trans. William Barrett and Henry Aiken, in *The Existentialist Tradition*, ed. Nino Langiulli (Garden City, NY: Doubleday, 1971), p. 229.

40. The historical details and the meaning of Heidegger's connection to the Nazis is the subject of a vast literature. For a succinct review of the issues and an introduction to the debates see Ian Thompson, "Heidegger and National Socialism," in *A Companion to Heidegger*, ed. Hubert L. Dreyfus and Mark A. Wrathall (Malden, MA: Blackwell Publishing, 2005).

41. Henry Corbin, *Avicenna and the Visionary Recital*, trans. W. Trask, Bollingen Series LXVI (Princeton NJ: Princeton University Press, 1960), p. 4.

42. Henry Corbin, *En Islam Iranien: Aspects spirituels et philosophiques, Tome. IV: L'Ecole d'Ispahan - L'Ecole Shaykhie - Le Douzieme Imam* (Paris: Gallimard, Bibliothèque des Idees, 1973), p. 410.

43. Henry Corbin, *En Islam Iranien: Aspects spirituels et philosophiques, Tome III: Les fideles d'amour et Shi'isme et sufisme* (Paris: Gallimard, Bibliothèque des Idees, 1972), p. 15 ff.

44. Henry Corbin, "The *Imago Templi* in Confrontation with Secular Norms," in *Temple and Contemplation*, trans. P. Sherrard and L. Sherrard (London: Kegan Paul International, 1986), p. 388, italics in original.

45. C. S. Lewis, *The Voyage of the Dawn Treader* (New York: Macmillan, 1952).

46. Corbin, *Avicenna*, p. 159.

47. Corbin, *Les fideles d'amour et Shi'isme et sufisme*, p. 16.

48. For what follows, see *Ibid.*, esp. Livre III.

49. Carl Ernst says that Corbin's translation of *iltibas* as "ambiguity" does not do justice to the rich nuances of the word. It suggests "clothing with divinity" as well as "covering up" and "confusion." See Carl Ernst, *Words of Ecstasy in Sufism* (Albany, N.Y.: State University of New York Press, 1985), p. 149, n. 36.

50. For example see Paul Evdokimov, *The Art of the Icon: A Theology of Beauty* (Crestwood, NY: St. Vladimir's Seminary Press, 1990).

51. Denis de Rougemont, *Love in the Western World*, trans. Montgomery Belgion, rev. ed., with Postscript (Princeton, NJ: Princeton University Press, 1983).

52. *Ibid.*, pp. 61-62, italics in original.
53. *Ibid.*, pp. 63-64, italics in original.
54. *Ibid.*, p. 69, italics in original.
55. *Ibid.*, p. 310, italics in original.
56. *Ibid.*, p. 311.
57. *Ibid.*, p. 368.
58. *Ibid.*, pp. 377-378.
59. *Ibid.*, p. 309.
60. In a letter to Corbin, in *Henry Corbin*, ed. Christian Jambet, Cahier de l'Herne, no. 39. Consacré à Henry Corbin, Paris, 1981, 341.
61. Henry Corbin, "The Jasmine of the *Fedeli d'Amore*: A Discourse on Ruzbehan Baqli of Shiraz," *Sphinx 3: A Journal for Archetypal Psychology and the Arts* (1990): 208.
62. Corbin, *Avicenna*, p. 116.
63. Corbin, *Spiritual Body*, pp. 9-10.
64. Henry Corbin, "De la théologie apophatique comme antidote du nihilisme," in *Le Paradoxe du Monothèisme* (Paris: Ed. de l'Herne/Le Livre de Poche, 1981), p. 203, italics in original.
65. Corbin, *Spiritual Body*, p. 42.
66. Olivier Clément, *On Being Human: A Spiritual Anthropology* (New York: New City Press, 2000), p. 58.
67. Michael Auping, *Anselm Kiefer: Heaven and Earth* (Fort Worth, TX: Modern Art Museum of Fort Worth in association with Prestel, 2005), p. 27.
68. Corbin, "De la théologie apophatique," p. 205.
69. Dietrich Bonhoeffer, *Letters and Papers from Prison* (New York: Macmillan, 1967), p. 300.
70. Paul Celan, *Selected Poems and Prose of Paul Celan*, trans. John Felstiner (New York: W. W. Norton, 2001), p. 396.
71. Celan was profoundly immersed in the works of Martin Heidegger. The philosopher's probing and seminal writings on the meaning and nature of poetic language had a powerful fascination for the poet. And yet, as we have seen, his search implied an allegiance to a vision of humanity that was in the end trans-human, and uncomfortably close to the inhuman. Yet there was something so attractive to Celan in Heidegger's vision that his tortured relationship with the thinker and his work never came to a resolution. See James K. Lyon, *Paul Celan and Martin Heidegger: An Unresolved Conversation, 1951-1970* (Baltimore, MD: Johns Hopkins University Press, 2006).
72. Uwe Poerksen, *Plastic Words: The Tyranny of a Modular Language*, trans. Jutta Mason and David Cayley (University Park, PA: The Pennsylvania State University Press, 1995) provides a particularly fine analysis of this.

73. Celan, *Selected Poems*, pp. 395-396.
74. Corbin, *Creative Imagination*, p. 248.

CHAPTER SEVEN: A PERSONAL STORY

1. Henry Corbin, "Iranian Studies and Philosophy," in *The Voyage and the Messenger: Iran and Philosophy*, trans. Joseph Rowe (Berkeley, CA: North Atlantic Books, 1998), p. 81.
2. James Hillman, *The Thought of the Heart and the Soul of the World* (Dallas, TX: Spring Publications, 1992), p. 3.
3. Henry Corbin, *Avicenna and the Visionary Recital*, trans. W. Trask, Bollingen Series LXVI (Princeton, NJ: Princeton University Press, 1960), p. 6.
4. I have adopted Rustom's translation of this last title. See Mohammed Rustom, "The Symbology of the Wing in Suhrawardi's *The Reverberation of Gabriel's Wing*," *Transcendent Philosophy* 7 (2006): 189-202.
5. Corbin, *Avicenna*, p. 4.
6. *Ibid.*, p. 33.
7. *Ibid.*, p. 32, italics in original.
8. *Ibid.*, p. 35.
9. Henry Corbin, "Destin comparé de la philosophie iranienne après Averrroës," in *Philosophie iranienne et philosophie comparé* (Tehran: Académie Impériale Iranienne de Philosophie, 1977), p. 138.
10. Angelus Silesius, *The Cherubinic Wanderer, Selections*, trans. and intro. J. E. Crawford Flitch (London, 1932), I, 8, quoted in Corbin, *Avicenna*, p. 130. The translators of Corbin's *Avicenna* used the Trask translation [Angelus Silesius, *The Cherubinic Wanderer, Selections*, trans. Willard R. Trask, intro. Curt von Faber du Faur (New York: Pantheon Books, 1953)]. I prefer Crawford Flitch's renderings and have used them here instead of the translations used in the English versions of Corbin's works.
11. *Ibid.*, I, 100, quoted in Corbin, *Avicenna*, p. 314.
12. *Ibid.*, II, 178, quoted in Corbin, *Avicenna*, p. 314.
13. *Ibid.*, II, 102 and I, 23, quoted in Henry Corbin, "Le Récit d'Initiation et l'Hermétism en Iran," in *L'Homme et Son Ange: Initiation et Chevalerie Spirituelle* (Paris: Fayard, 1983), p. 74.
14. Corbin, "Destin comparé," p. 136.
15. From a letter by Rilke to his Polish translator, Witold von Hulewicz, November 13, 1925, in Rainer Maria Rilke, *Letters of Rainer Maria Rilke 1910-1926*, trans. Jane Bannard Greene and M. D. Herter Norton (New York: W. W. Norton & Company, 1947), pp. 375-376. Portions of this letter are quoted in Corbin's *Avicenna* (pp. 136-137) from the French edition of Rilke's correspondence.

16. *Ibid.*, p. 136.
17. Corbin, "Destin comparé," pp. 136-137.
18. See The Qur'an, Sura XVIII and Henry Corbin, *Alone with the Alone: Creative Imagination in the Sufism of Ibn 'Arabi*, trans. R. Manheim, Bollingen Series XCI (Princeton, NJ: Princeton University Press, 1997), pp. 55ff. (Hereafter referred to as *Creative Imagination*.)
19. Rainer Maria Rilke, *The Selected Poetry of Rainer Maria Rilke*, ed. and trans. Stephen Mitchell (New York: Random House/Vintage, 1989), p. 199.
20. Corbin, *Creative Imagination*, p. 134.
21. *Ibid.*, p. 292.
22. This apt turn of phrase is from *Radical Orthodoxy: A New Theology*, ed. John Milbank, Catherine Pickstock, and Graham Ward (London: Routledge, 1999), p. 4.
23. Rilke, *Selected Poetry*, pp. 199-200.
24. Letter to von Hulewicz in Rilke, *Letters*, p. 374.
25. Rilke, *Selected Poetry*, p. 201.
26. *Ibid.*, p. 201.
27. William Carlos Williams, "Asphodel, That Greeny Flower," in *Selected Poems of William Carlos Williams*, intro. Randall Jarrell (New York: New Directions, 1968), pp. 150-151.
28. Shihâboddîn Yahyâ Sohravardi, *L'Archange empourpré: Quinze Traités et récits mystiques—Présentés et annotés par Henry Corbin* (Paris: Fayard, 1976), p. 108.
29. René Char, "Comment vivre sans inconnu devant soi?" in *Selected Poems*, ed. Mary Ann Caws and Tina Jolas (New York: New Directions, 1992), p. 38.
30. Rainer Maria Rilke, "Ninth Elegy," in *Selected Poetry*, p. 199.
31. Angelus Silesius, VI, 263, quoted in James E. Irby, "Introduction," in *Other Inquisitions: 1937-1952*, by Jorge Luis Borges, trans. Ruth L. C. Simms (New York: Simon and Schuster, 1968), p. xv. This distich also appears in the original German as the final epigraph in *Other Inquisitions* (p. 188).

Bibliography

Abram, David. *The Spell of the Sensuous: Perception and Language in a More-Than-Human World.* New York: Pantheon, 1996.

Al~xander, Christopher. *The Nature of Order: An Essay on the Art of Building and the Nature of the Universe. Book One: The Phenomenon of Life.* New York: Oxford University Press, 2001.

_____. *The Nature of Order: An Essay on the Art of Building and the Nature of the Universe. Book Two: The Process of Creating Life.* Berkeley, CA: The Center for Environmental Structure, 2002.

Auping, Michael. *Anselm Kiefer. Heaven and Earth.* Fort Worth, TX: Modern Art Museum of Fort Worth, in association with Prestel, 2005.

Besançon, Alain. *The Forbidden Image: An Intellectual History of Iconoclasm.* Trans. Jane Marie Todd. Chicago: University of Chicago Press, 2000.

Blake, William. *The Poems of William Blake.* Ed. W. H. Stevenson. Text by David Erdman. New York: W.W. Norton, 1971.

Bloom, Harold. *Omens of Millennium: The Gnosis of Angels, Dreams and Resurrection.* New York: Riverhead Books, 1997.

_____. "Preface." In *Alone with the Alone: Creative Imagination in the Sufism of Ibn 'Arabi.* By Henry Corbin. Trans. R. Manheim. Bollingen Series XCI. Princeton, NJ: Princeton University Press, 1997.

_____. *Shakespeare: The Invention of the Human.* New York: Riverhead Books, 1998.

Bonhoeffer, Dietrich. *Letters and Papers from Prison.* New York: Macmillan, 1967.

Boyarin, Daniel. *Border Lines: The Partition of Judeo-Christianity.* Philadelphia, PA: University of Pennsylvania Press, 2004.

Brentano, Franz. "Nous Poiêtikos: Survey of Earlier Interpretations." In *Essays on Aristotle's De Anima.* Ed. M. Nussbaum and A. Rorty. Oxford, UK: Clarendon Press, 1992, pp. 313-341.

Brown, Norman O. "The Apocalypse of Islam." In *Apocalypse &/or Metamorphosis.* Berkeley, CA: University of California Press, 1991.

Butler, Samuel. *Erewhon and Erewhon Revisited.* New York: Modern Library, 1955.

Carrell, Peter R. *Jesus and the Angels: Angelology and the Christology of the Apocalypse of John.* Cambridge, UK: Cambridge University Press, 1997.

Caston, Victor. "Aristotle's Two Intellects: A Modest Proposal." *Phronesis* 44, no. 3 (1999): 199-227.

Cayley, David. *Ivan Illich: In Conversation.* Concord, Ont.: Anansi Press, 1992.

_____. *Rivers North of the Future: The Testament of Ivan Illich as told to David Cayley.* Toronto: Anansi Press, 2005.

Celan, Paul. *Selected Poems and Prose of Paul Celan.* Trans. John Felstiner. New York: W. W. Norton, 2001.

Char, René. *Selected Poems.* Ed. Mary Ann Caws and Tina Jolas. New York: New Directions, 1992.

Cheetham, Tom. *Green Man, Earth Angel: The Prophetic Tradition and the Battle for the Soul of the World.* SUNY Series in the Western Esoteric Tradition. Albany, NY: State University of New York Press, 2005.

_____. *The World Turned Inside Out: Henry Corbin and Islamic Mysticism.* New Orleans, LA: Spring Journal Books, 2003.

Chittick, William. *Imaginal Worlds: Ibn al-'Arabi and the Problem of Religious Diversity.* Albany, NY: State University of New York Press, 1994.

_____. *The Self-Disclosure of God: Principles of Ibn 'Arabi's Cosmology.* Albany, NY: State University of New York Press, 1998.

Chryssavgis, John. *In the Heart of the Desert: The Spirituality of the Desert Fathers and Mothers.* Bloomington, IN: World Wisdom, 2003.

Clément, Olivier. *The Roots of Christian Mysticism: Texts From the Patristic Era with Commentary.* London: New City Press, 1993.

_____. *On Being Human: A Spiritual Anthropology.* New York: New City Press, 2000.

Cohen, Richard A. *Ethics, Exegesis and Philosophy: Interpretation after Levinas.* Cambridge, UK: Cambridge University Press, 2001.

_____. "Introduction." In *Humanism of the Other.* By Emmanuel Levinas. Trans. Nidra Poller. Urbana, IL: University of Illinois, 2003.

Corbin, Henry. *Alone with the Alone: Creative Imagination in the Sufism of Ibn 'Arabi.* Trans. R. Manheim. Bollingen Series XCI. Princeton, NJ: Princeton University Press, 1997. Originally published as *Creative Imagination in the Sufism of Ibn 'Arabi,* 1969.

_____. *Avicenna and the Visionary Recital.* Trans. W. Trask. Bollingen Series LXVI. Princeton, NJ: Princeton University Press, 1960.

_____. "De la théologie apophatique comme antidote du nihilisme." In *Le Paradoxe du Monothèisme.* Paris: Ed. de l'Herne/Le Livre de Poche, 1981.

_____. "Destin comparé de la philosophie iranienne après Averroës." In *Philosophie iranienne et philosophie comparé.* Tehran: Académie Impériale Iranienne de Philosophie, 1977.

_____. "Divine Epiphany and Spiritual Birth in Ismailian Gnosis." In *Cyclical Time and Ismaili Gnosis.* Trans. Ralph Manheim and James W. Morris. London: Kegan Paul International, 1983.

_____. *En Islam Iranien: Aspects spirituels et philosophiques, Tome I : Le shi'isme duodècemain.* Paris: Gallimard, Bibliothéque des Idees, 1971.

_____. *En Islam Iranien: Aspects spirituels et philosophiques, Tome II: Sohrawardi et les platoniciens de perse*. Paris: Gallimard, Bibliothéque des Idees, 1971.

_____. *En Islam Iranien: Aspects spirituels et philosophiques, Tome III: Les fideles d'amour et Shi'isme et sufisme*. Paris: Gallimard, Bibliothéque des Idees, 1972.

_____. *En Islam Iranien: Aspects spirituels et philosophiques, Tome IV: L'Ecole d'Ispahan - L'Ecole Shaykhie - Le Douzieme Imam*. Paris: Gallimard, Bibliothéque des Idees, 1973.

_____. "Eyes of Flesh and Eyes of Fire: Science and Gnosis." *Material for Thought* 8 (1980): 5-10.

_____. "From the Gnosis of Antiquity to Ismaili Gnosis." In *Cyclical Time and Ismaili Gnosis*. Trans. Ralph Manheim and James W. Morris. London: Kegan Paul International, 1983.

_____. "Iranian Studies and Philosophy." In *The Voyage and the Messenger: Iran and Philosophy*. Trans. Joseph Rowe. Berkeley, CA: North Atlantic Books, 1998. Originally published as *L'Iran et La Philosophie*, Fayard, 1990.

_____. "L'Initiation Ismaèlienne ou l'Esoterisme et le Verbe." In *L'Homme et Son Ange: Initiation et Chevalerie Spirituelle*. Paris: Fayard, 1983, pp. 81-205.

_____. "Le paradoxe du monothèisme." In *Le Paradoxe du Monothèisme*. Paris: Ed. de l'Herne/Le Livre de Poche, 1981.

_____. "Le Récit d'Initiation et l'Hermétism en Iran." In *L'Homme et Son Ange: Initiation et Chevalerie Spirituelle*. Paris: Fayard, 1983.

_____. "*Mundus Imaginalis* or the Imaginary and the Imaginal." In *Swedenborg and Esoteric Islam*. Trans. L. Fox. West Chester, PA : Swedenborg Foundation, 1995.

_____. "Preface : Harmonia Abrahamica." In *Évangile de Barnabé: Recherches sur la composition et l'origine*. By Luigi Cirillo and Michel Frémaux. Paris: Éditions Beauchesne, 1977, pp. 5-17.

_____. "Prefatory Letter." In *The New Polytheism*. By David Miller. Dallas: Spring Publications, 1981.

_____. *Spiritual Body and Celestial Earth: From Mazdean Iran to Shi'ite Iran*. Trans. N. Pearson. Bollingen Series XCI: 2. Princeton, NJ: Princeton University Press, 1977. (5th Printing, 1989, with "Prelude to the Second Edition: Towards a Chart of the Imaginal").

_____. "The Configuration of the Temple of the Ka'bah as the Secret of the Spiritual Life." In *Temple and Contemplation*. Trans. P. Sherrard and L. Sherrard. London: Kegan Paul International, 1986.

_____. "The *Imago Templi* in Confrontation with Secular Norms." In *Temple and Contemplation*. Trans. P. Sherrard and L. Sherrard. London: Kegan Paul International, 1986.

_____. "The Jasmine of the *Fedeli d'Amore*: A Discourse on Ruzbehan Baqli of Shiraz." *Sphinx 3: A Journal for Archetypal Psychology and the Arts* (1994): 189-223.

_____. *The Man of Light in Iranian Sufism.* Trans. N. Pearson. New Lebanon, NY: Omega Publications, 1994.

_____. "Theophanies and Mirrors: Idols or Icons?" Trans. Jane Pratt and A. K. Donohue. *Spring* (1983): 1-2.

Cranz, F. Edward. *Reorientations of Western Thought from Antiquity to the Renaissance.* Ed. Nancy Streuver. London, W. H. Smith, 2006.

_____. "The Reorientation of Western Thought c.1100 A.D.: The Break with the Ancient Tradition and Its Consequences for Renaissance and Reformation." Unpublished paper delivered at the Duke University Center for Medieval and Renaissance Studies, March 24, 1982.

cummings, e. e. *A Miscellany / Revised.* Ed. George J. Firmage. New York: October House, 1965.

de Rougemont, Denis, "Hérétiques des toutes les religions ...." In *Henry Corbin.* Ed. Christian Jambet. Cahier de l'Herne, no. 39. Consacré à Henry Corbin. Paris: Ed. de l'Herne, 1981.

_____. *Love in the Western World.* Trans. Montgomery Belgion. Rev. ed. with Postscript. Princeton, NJ: Princeton University Press, 1983.

Deck, John. *Nature, Contemplation and the One: A Study in the Philosophy of Plotinus.* Toronto: University of Toronto Press, 1967.

Diamond, Stanley. *In Search of the Primitive: A Critique of Civilization.* London: Transaction, 1974.

Dôgen. *Moon in a Dewdrop: Writings of Zen Master Dôgen.* Ed. Kazuaki Tanahashi. New York: North Point, 1985.

Ehrman, Bart D. *Lost Christianities: The Battles for Scripture and the Faiths We Never Knew.* Oxford, UK: Oxford University Press, 2003.

Ernst, Carl W. *Words of Ecstasy in Sufism.* Albany, NY: State University of New York Press, 1985.

Evdokimov, Paul. *Ages of the Spiritual Life.* Crestwood, NY: St. Vladimir's Seminary Press, 1998.

_____. *The Art of the Icon: A Theology of Beauty.* Crestwood, NY: St. Vladimir's Seminary Press, 1990.

Fletcher-Louis, Crispin H. T. *Luke-Acts: Angels, Christology and Soteriology.* Tubingen: J. C. B. Mohr, 1997.

Friedman, Michael. *A Parting of the Ways: Carnap, Cassirer and Heidegger.* Chicago, IL: Open Court, 2000.

Hampson, Daphne. "Luther on the Self: A Feminist Critique." In *Feminist Theology: A Reader.* Ed. Ann Loades. Louisville, KY: Westminster/John Knox Press, 1990, pp. 215-225.

Hannah, Darrell D. *Michael and Christ: Michael Traditions and Angel Christology in Early Christianity.* Tübingen: Mohr Siebeck, 1999.

Heidegger, Martin. "Letter On Humanism." Trans. William Barrett and Henry Aiken. In *The Existentialist Tradition.* Ed. Nino Langiulli. Garden City, NY: Doubleday, 1971.

Hillman, James. *A Blue Fire: Selected Writings by James Hillman*. Ed. and intro.
Thomas Moore. New York: Harper Collins, 1989.

_____. *Archetypal Psychology*. Uniform Edition of the Writings of James
Hillman. Vol. 1. Putnam, CT: Spring Publications, 2004.

_____. *Kinds of Power: A Guide to Its Intelligent Uses*. New York: Doubleday,
1995.

_____. "On the Necessity of Abnormal Psychology." In *Facing the Gods*. Dallas,
TX: Spring Publications, 1980.

_____. "Psychology: Monotheistic or Polytheistic?" *Spring* (1971): 193-208.

_____. "Psychology: Monotheistic or Polytheistic: Twenty Five Years Later."
Spring 60 (1996): 111-25.

_____. *Re-Visioning Psychology*. New York: Harper & Row, 1975.

_____. *The Thought of the Heart and the Soul of the World*. Dallas, TX: Spring
Publications, 1992.

Hoinacki, Lee. "Reading Ivan Illich." In *The Challenges of Ivan Illich: A Collective
Reflection*. Ed. Lee Hoinacki and Carl Mitcham. Albany, NY: State
Uunivesity of New York Press, 2002, pp. 1-7.

Illich, Ivan. *H₂O and the Waters of Forgetfulness: Reflections on the Historicity of
Stuff*. Dallas, TX: Dallas Institute of Art and Humanities, 1984.

_____. *In the Vineyard of the Text: A Commentary to Hugh's Didascalicon*.
Chicago, IL: University of Chicago Press, 1993.

_____. "The Loss of World and Flesh." Trans. Muska Nagel and Barbara
Duden. Thinking after Ilich. Website of the Circle for Research on
Proportionality. 2007. <http://www.pudel.uni-bremen.de/pdf/
IllichBecker_en.pdf>. Originally published in German as "Verlust von Welt
und Fleisch," in *Freitag* 51, no. 13 (December 2002): 18.

_____. "The Rebirth of Epimethean Man." In *Deschooling Society*. New York:
Harper, 1971.

_____. "The Scopic Past and the Ethics of the Gaze: A Plea for the Historical
Study of Ocular Perception." Ivan Illich Archives. Personal website of
David Tinapple. 2002. <http://www.davidtinapple.com/illich/
1998_scopic_past.PDF>.

Inchausti, Robert. *Thomas Merton's American Prophecy*. Albany, NY: State
University of New York Press, 1998.

Irby, James. "Introduction." In *Other Inquisitions 1937-1952*. By Jorge Luis
Borges. Trans. Ruth L. C. Simms. New York: Simon and Schuster, 1968.

Jambet, Christian, ed. *Henry Corbin*. Cahier de l'Herne, no. 39. Consacré à
Henry Corbin. Paris: Ed. de l'Herne, 1981.

_____. *The Act of Being: The Philosophy of Revelation in Mullâ Sadrâ*. Trans.
Jeff Fort. New York: Zone Books, 2006.

James, M. R. *The Apocryphal New Testament*. Oxford, UK: Oxford University
Press, 1950.

Jung, C. G. *The Collected Works of C. G. Jung.* Trans. R. F. C. Hull. Bollingen
  Series XX, Princeton, NJ: Princeton University Press, 1970.

Kapleau, Philip. *Three Pillars of Zen: Teaching, Practice and Enlightenment.* New
  ed. New York: Anchor Books, 1989.

Kavanagh, Aidan. *On Liturgical Theology.* Collegeville, MN: The Liturgical
  Press, 1984.

King, Karen L. *What Is Gnosticism?* Cambridge, MA: Harvard University Press,
  2003.

Lawrence, D. H. *The Letters of D. H. Lawrence, Vol. 5.* Ed. James T. Boulton
  and Lindeth Vasey. Cambridge, UK: Cambridge University Press, 1989.

Lewis, C. S. *The Voyage of the Dawn Treader.* New York: Macmillan, 1952.

Lyon, James K. *Paul Celan and Martin Heidegger: An Unresolved Conversation,
  1951-1970.* Baltimore, MD: Johns Hopkins University Press, 2006.

Merleau-Ponty, Maurice. *The Visible and the Invisible.* Evanston, IL:
  Northwestern University Press, 1968.

Merton, Thomas. *Seeds.* Ed. and intro. Robert Inchausti. Boston, MA:
  Shambhala, 2002.

_____. *Thomas Merton, Spiritual Master: The Essential Writings.* Ed. Lawrence
  S. Cunningham. New York: Paulist Press, 1992.

Milbank, John, Catherine Pickstock, and Graham Ward, eds. *Radical
  Orthodoxy: A New Theology.* London: Routledge, 1999.

Miles, Margaret R. *Carnal Knowing: Female Nakedness and Religious Meaning
  in the Christian West.* Boston, MA: Beacon Press, 1989.

_____. *Fullness of Life: Historical Foundations for a New Asceticism.* Philadelphia,
  PA: Westminster Press, 1981.

Miller, David L. *The New Polytheism.* Dallas, TX: Spring Publications, 1981.

Nasr, Seyyed Hossein. *Ideals and Realities of Islam.* London: Allen & Unwin,
  1966.

_____. "Oral Transmission and the Book in Islamic Education: The Spoken
  and the Written Word." In *The Book in the Islamic World: The Written Word
  and Communication in the Middle East.* Ed. George N. Atiyeh. Albany,
  NY: State University of New York Press, 1995, pp. 57-70.

Nellas, Panayiotis. *Deification in Christ: Orthodox Perspectives on the Nature of
  the Human Person.* Trans. Norman Russell. Crestwood, NY: St. Vladimir's
  Seminary Press, 1987.

Partridge, Eric. *Origins: A Short Dictionary of English Etymology.* New York:
  Macmillan, 1966.

Plotinus. *Plotinus: The Enneads.* Trans. Stephen MacKenna. Burdett, NY:
  Larson Publications, 1992.

Poerksen, Uwe. *Plastic Words: The Tyranny of a Modular Language.* Trans. Jutta
  Mason and David Cayley. University Park, PA: The Pennsylvania State
  University Press, 1995.

Quigley, Thomas, "News Briefs." *Catholic News Service, U.S.* December 10, 2002.

Ra lin, Paul. *Primitve Man as Philosopher.* New York: Dover, 1957.

Rilke, Rainer Maria. *Letters of Rainer Maria Rilke 1910-1926.* Trans. Jane Bannard Greene and M. D. Herter Norton. New York: W. W. Norton & Company, 1947.

_____. *Selected Poems of Rainer Maria Rilke. A Translation from the German and Commentary by Robert Bly.* New York: Harper and Row, 1981.

_____. *The Selected Poetry of Rainer Maria Rilke.* Ed. and trans. Stephen Mitchell. New York: Random House/Vintage, 1989.

Rosenbaum, Ron. *The Shakespeare Wars: Clashing Scholars, Public Fiascoes, Palace Coups.* New York: Random House, 2006.

Rothenberg, J. and Pierre Joris, eds. *Poems for the Millennium: The University of California Book of Modern and Postmodern Poetry, Vol. 2: From Postwar to Millennium.* Berkeley, CA: University of California Press, 1998.

Rustom, Mohammed. "The Symbology of the Wing in Suhrawardi's *The Reverberation of Gabriel's Wing." Transcendent Philosophy* 7 (2006): 189-202.

Sells, Michael. *Approaching the Qu'ran: The Early Revelations.* Ashland, OR: White Cloud Press, 1999.

_____. *Mystical Languages of Unsaying.* Chicago, IL: University of Chicago Press, 1994.

Sherrard, Philip. *Christianity: Lineaments of a Sacred Tradition.* Brookline, MA: Holy Cross Orthodox Press, 1998.

Sohravardi, Shihâboddîn Yahyâ. *L'Archange empourpré: Quinze Traités et récits mystiques. Présentés et annotés par Henry Corbin.* Paris: Fayard, 1976.

Silesius, Angelus. *The Cherubinic Wanderer, Selections.* Trans. and intro. J. E. Crawford Flitch. London, 1932. The Internet Sacred Text Archive. 2007. <http://www.sacred-texts.com/chr/sil/scw/index.htm>.

_____. *The Cherubinic Wanderer, Selections.* Trans. Willard R. Trask. Intro. Curt von Faber du Faur. New York: Pantheon Books, 1953.

Simon, Gérard. *Le regard, l'être et l'apparence dans l'optique de l'antiquité.* Paris: Éditions du Seuil, 1988.

Snyder, Gary. *The Real Work: Interviews and Talks 1964-1979.* New York: New Directions, 1980.

Steiner, George. *Real Presences.* Chicago, IL: University of Chicago Press, 1989.

Subtelny, Maria E. "History and Religion: The Fallacy of Metaphysical Questions (A Review Article)." *Iranian Studies* 36, no. 1 (March 2003): 91-101.

Suzuki, Shunryu. *Zen Mind, Beginner's Mind.* New York: Weatherhill, 1970.

Thompson, Iain. "Heidegger and National Socialism." In *A Companion to Heidegger.* Ed. Hubert L. Dreyfus and Mark A. Wrathall. Malden, MA: Blackwell Publishing, 2005.

Todd, Andrew and Franco La Cecla. "Ivan Illich." *The Guardian.* December 9, 2002, p. 22.

Tranströmer, Tomas. *Selected Poems: 1954-1986.* Ed. Robert Hass. Hopewell, N.J.: Ecco Press, 1987.

Von Franz, Marie-Louise, ed. *Aurora Consurgens: A Document Attributed to Thomas Aquinas on the Problem of Opposites in Alchemy.* Trans. R. F. C. Hull and A. S. B. Glover. Torono: Inner City Books, 2000.

Wasserstrom, Stephen M. *Religion After Religion: Gershom Scholem, Mircea Eliade and Henry Corbin at Eranos.* Princeton, NJ: Princeton University Press, 1999.

Whitman, Walt. *Leaves of Grass.* Ed. Sculley Bradley and Harold Blodgett. New York: W. W. Norton, 1973.

Williams, William Carlos. *Selected Poems of William Carlos Williams.* Intro. Randall Jarrell. New York : New Directions, 1968.

Index

SPRING JOURNAL BOOKS

The book publishing imprint of *Spring Journal,*
the oldest Jungian psychology journal in the world

STUDIES IN ARCHETYPAL PSYCHOLOGY SERIES
Series Editor: Greg Mogenson

Collected English Papers, Wolfgang Giegerich
  Vol. 1: *The Neurosis of Psychology: Primary Papers Towards a Critical Psychology,* ISBN 978-1-882670-42-6, 284 pp., $20.00
  Vol. 2: *Technology and the Soul: From the Nuclear Bomb to the World Wide Web,* ISBN 978-1-882670-43-4, 356 pp., $25.00
  Vol. 3: *Soul-Violence* ISBN 978-1-882670-44-2
  Vol. 4: *The Soul Always Thinks* ISBN 978-1-882670-45-0

Dialectics & Analytical Psychology: The El Capitan Canyon Seminar, Wolfgang Giegerich, David L. Miller, and Greg Mogenson, ISBN 978-1-882670-92-2, 136 pp., $20.00

Northern Gnosis: Thor, Baldr, and the Volsungs in the Thought of Freud and Jung, Greg Mogenson, ISBN 978-1-882670-90-6, 140 pp., $20.00

Raids on the Unthinkable: Freudian and Jungian Psychoanalyses, Paul Kugler, ISBN 978-1-882670-91-4, 160 pp., $20.00

The Essentials of Style: A Handbook for Seeing and Being Seen, Benjamin Sells, ISBN 978-1-882670-68-X, 141 pp., $21.95

The Wounded Researcher: A Depth Psychological Approach to Research, Robert Romanyshyn, ISBN 978-1-882670-47-7

The Sunken Quest, the Wasted Fisher, the Pregnant Fish: Postmodern Reflections on Depth Psychology, Ronald Schenk, ISBN 978-1-882670-48-5, $20.00

Fire in the Stone: The Alchemy of Desire, Stanton Marlan, ed., ISBN 978-1-882670-49-3, 206 pp., $22.95

Honoring David L. Miller

Disturbances in the Field: Essays in Honor of David L. Miller, Christine Downing, ed., ISBN 978-1-882670-37-X, 318 pp., $23.95

The David L. Miller Trilogy

Three Faces of God: Traces of the Trinity in Literature and Life, David L. Miller, ISBN 978-1-882670-94-9, 197 pp., $20.00

Christs: Meditations on Archetypal Images in Christian Theology, David L. Miller, ISBN 978-1-882670-93-0, 249 pp., $20.00

Hells and Holy Ghosts: A Theopoetics of Christian Belief, David L. Miller, ISBN 978-1-882670-99-3, 238 pp., $20.00

The Electra Series

Electra: Tracing a Feminine Myth through the Western Imagination, Nancy Cater, ISBN 978-1-882670-98-1, 137 pp., $20.00

Fathers' Daughters: Breaking the Ties That Bind, Maureen Murdock, ISBN 978-1-882670-31-0, 258 pp., $20.00

Daughters of Saturn: From Father's Daughter to Creative Woman, Patricia Reis, ISBN 978-1-882670-32-9, 361 pp., $23.95

Women's Mysteries: Twoard a Poetics of Gender, Christine Downing, ISBN 978-1-882670-99-XX, 237 pp., $20.00

Gods in Our Midst: Mythological Images of the Masculine—A Woman's View, Christine Downing, ISBN 978-1-882670-28-0, 152 pp., $20.00

Journey through Menopause: A Personal Rite of Passage, Christine Downing, ISBN 978-1-882670-33-7, 172 pp., $20.00

Portrait of the Blue Lady: The Character of Melancholy, Lyn Cowan, ISBN 978-1-882670-96-5, 314 pp., $23.95
